TROPICAL
MODERNISM

TROPICAL MODERNISM

Architecture and Independence

Christopher Turner

V&A Publishing

First published by V&A Publishing to accompany the exhibition *Tropical Modernism: Architecture and Independence* on view from 2 March to 22 September 2024 at the Victoria and Albert Museum, South Kensington, London SW7 2RL

Supported by James Bartos and Celia and Edward Atkin CBE

With further support from The Estate of Mrs Hilda Rose Carloss

This publication is supported by the Graham Foundation

Distributed in North America by Abrams, an imprint of ABRAMS

The moral right of the authors has been asserted.

ISBN 978 1 83851 055 8

10 9 8 7 6 5 4 3 2 1
2028 2027 2026 2025 2024

A catalogue record for this book is available from the British Library.

V&A Publishing

Supporting the world's leading museum of art and design, the Victoria and Albert Museum, London

Interviews with Ola Uduku, Samia Nkrumah, Vikramaditya Prakash, Jeet Malhotra, Henry Wellington, John Owusu Addo, Ram Rahman and Raj Rewal were conducted by Christopher Turner between 2019 and 2024, and transcribed and edited for this publication.

Front cover: A shop assistant at the Sick-Hagemeyer store in Accra photographed by James Barnor, 1971
Back cover: Students at Kwame Nkrumah University of Science and Technology (KNUST) Department of Architecture building Buckminster Fuller-inspired geodesic structures, 1960s
Frontispiece: Unity Hall, KNUST, Kumasi by John Owuso Addo and Miro Marasović, 1967
Opposite Foreword: The V&A exhibition *Tropical Modernism: Architecture and Independence*, 2024

Designer: (studio) Boris Meister
Copyeditor: Neil Stewart
Proofreader: Jessica Spencer
Indexer: Nic Nicholas

Printed and bound in Wales by Gomer Press
Repro by Dexter Premedia Ltd

Foreword

Tristram Hunt
Director, V&A

Architecture was one of the foundational subject areas for the V&A. Our earliest acquisitions included ornamental details from Renaissance architecture, and the Cast Courts were first opened in 1873 as the Architectural Courts, to house monumental reproductions of great architecture from across the world. *Tropical Modernism: Architecture and Independence* offers a chance to develop this vital aspect of the museum's mission for new audiences interested in the history of architectural exchange between the Global North and South.

For this is an exhibition that examines the architecture of Tropical Modernism, a style of western import that dominated British colonies and former colonies, specifically Ghana and India, from the 1940s to the '60s. But it is also an account of how this imperial design was reimagined once those countries gained independence, and how local architects appropriated and adapted it as a form of post-colonial nationhood. Architecture that had once served as a vehicle of colonial ideology became a symbol of nascent political freedom, distinct from its foundations. As an elemental part of the V&A's collection was born of the colonial moment, it becomes even more vital to understand this contested heritage of colonialism, with all its implications for our multicultural present.

Central to the 2024 *Tropical Modernism* exhibition (see opposite) is a three-screen immersive film which debuted in a display at the 2023 Venice Architecture Biennale. It includes an interview with 95-year-old John Owusu Addo, one of Ghana's first qualified architects, whose name – like those of so many other indigenous practitioners – was never put to his work in the western record. This exhibition, and accompanying publication, seeks to give this pioneering generation of architects a previously denied voice. Their presence in this period of history is crucial both to the global story of architecture and design, and to our purpose as a museum.

We are grateful for the generous support of James Bartos and Celia and Edward Atkin CBE, and for the legacy gift from Mrs Hilda Rose Carloss, which made this exhibition possible. Thank you to the Graham Foundation for their support of this publication.

Architecture and Power in West Africa and India

(Previous spread) Nehru and Nkrumah
at the first Non-Aligned Movement
Summit in Belgrade, 1961

Drew and Fry with a
model for a West African
school, 1945

Introduction

In December 1958, when Ghana's prime minister Kwame Nkrumah landed at Delhi airport for a two-week visit of India, he was met by his Indian counterpart, Jawaharlal Nehru, and garlanded with flowers. The previous year, Ghana had won independence from the British – the first Sub-Saharan country in Africa to do so – after a decade-long campaign of 'civil disobedience' that had been inspired by Nehru and Mahatma Gandhi. In 1947 India had celebrated its own freedom from British colonial rule, and Nkrumah – who the Indian press referred to as the 'African Gandhi' – had much to learn from the country's post-colonial example.[1] He wanted to get Nehru's blessing for his plan to unite his continent into a United States of Africa and to be admitted to the club of non-aligned leaders.

Nkrumah was also interested in Indian architecture. He visited the new city of Chandigarh, the first Modernist city to be built from scratch, and some of India's innovative engineering projects, such as the Bhakra Nangal Dam in the Himalayas. These 'new temples of resurgent India', as Nehru described them, would inspire similar experiments in Ghana, as both leaders used Modernist architecture for nation-building and to shore up independence with programmes of rapid industrialization.[2] As Nkrumah boarded the train to Punjab, Nehru arrived late at the station to see him off, hurriedly getting out of his black velour coat as he ran towards him down the platform. He explained that his friend would need the coat in the cold mountainous region of northern India, but it was almost as if he was passing on the mantle.

In 1950 Nehru had invited architects Jane Drew and Maxwell Fry to build Chandigarh and they, in turn, invited Le Corbusier to help them design the new city. The British couple were, as Fry put it, 'coming straight from the easy glories of West Africa where we had reigned supreme'.[3] In the late 1940s, Drew and Fry had developed the tools of Tropical Modernism in British West Africa (now Gambia, Ghana, Sierra Leone and Nigeria), adapting a Modernist aesthetic that valued function over ornament to the hot, humid conditions of the region. Following independence, Nehru and Nkrumah commissioned major projects in this style, and a new generation of national architects more sensitive to local context gave birth to distinctive alternative Modernisms.

Tropical Modernism, despite its colonial associations, became an architectural symbol of a post-colonial future, symbolizing the utopian possibility of the transitional moment in which new freedoms were won.

Tropical Modernism was a late imperial architecture that might be seen to have been imposed on the Empire after the Second World War in large public and social projects that sought cynically to offset calls for independence, stimulate trade with Britain and create a new, modern colonial subject better able to produce goods for market and to buy them from Europe. Quick to dismiss traditional African architecture, in which they saw little of interest, Drew and Fry brought to West Africa what they described as a new, technological 'apparatus of thought'.[4] They built schools, colleges and other new institutions paid for by the Colonial Development and Welfare Act's £200m post-war programme (equivalent to £6 billion today) to reform, rebuild and modernize the colonies. Modernism was initially unpopular in Britain, and the region became something of a laboratory or playground for architects, presenting them with opportunities and commissions they would not have had at home; this led to British colonies being used as testing grounds for modes of construction and urban planning that then migrated back to the imperial centre.

Drew and Fry's many West African buildings had a distinctive language of climate control – with adjustable louvres, wide eaves and brise soleils that sometimes made superficial reference to the locality by incorporating African motifs – and attracted a great deal of international interest. This Tropical Modernism was perhaps Britain's unique (and colonial) architectural contribution to international Modernism: a scientifically informed, somewhat decorative style that belied contemporary criticism about the uniformity of modern architecture. Tropical Modernism, with its colonial assumptions and prejudices, was propagated through Drew and Fry's influential book *Tropical Architecture in the Humid Zone* (1956) and the Department of Tropical Architecture that they helped establish in 1954 at the Architectural Association (AA) in London, where they taught European architects to work in the colonies and trained a new generation of post-colonial architects.

Geoffrey Bawa, who trained at the AA and met Drew in 1959, was one of the few indigenous architects to be featured in a second edition of *Tropical Architecture* (1964), but no African architects were included. Like his colleague Minnette de Silva, Bawa rejected the 'veneer of modernism' that had entered his native Ceylon (now Sri Lanka).[5] He swamped his buildings – such as the Kandalama Hotel – in greenery, and his celebration of context, alternative aesthetics and craft traditions was an implicit critique of British colonial architecture and power. Today, stripped of its colonial associations, Tropical Modernism is experiencing something of a modish revival as an exotic and escapist style popular in verdant luxury hotels, bars and concrete jungle houses. But it has a problematic history and, through an examination of the context of British imperialism and decolonial struggle, this book (and related exhibition) seeks to show something of the politics behind the concrete.

'The history of the British Empire', as the writer and academic Priyamvada Gopal argues, 'is also the history of resistance to it'.[6] Just as Fry and Drew were starting work in West Africa, anti-colonial activists were meeting in 1945 at the 5th Pan-African Congress in Manchester where one of the organizers, Kwame Nkrumah, argued that revolutionary methods were required if Africa was to achieve independence. In 1947 he returned to the Gold Coast (now Ghana) and implemented a vigorous campaign of 'Positive Action' inspired by Gandhi and Nehru's successful freedom struggle in India. Tropical Modernism appeared against this background of decolonial struggle. Drew and Fry and their peers, despite their benevolent, paternalistic rhetoric, were building in the context of boycotts, strikes and riots, and their architecture was often a negotiation with this political landscape, used as an instrument of pacification against unrest.

Despite its colonial associations, Tropical Modernism was an important aspect of nation-building after independence in both India and Ghana, and it came to represent the internationalism and progressiveness of these new democratic countries, distinct from colonial culture. As these nations sought to improve local conditions with programmes of rapid industrialization, it was Tropical Modernism's apparent lack of ideology (certainly compared with

Minnette de Silva inspecting
concrete pillars in Colombo,
Ceylon (now Sri Lanka), 1951

The Kandalama Hotel by
Geoffrey Bawa, Dambulla,
Sri Lanka, 1994

earlier colonial architecture) and its promise of development and modernization, imagined as a form of neutral technical expertise, that made it so persuasive. But in truth, Tropical Modernism was deeply ideological, and it was both opposed by revivalist groups in the former colonies – who thought it a colonial imposition – and subverted and critiqued by those who embraced it.

Because there were relatively few indigenous architects, as the colonial system only recognized those who had gained qualifications abroad, many western architects bridged the transition and continued to find employment in post-colonial countries. In the early 1950s, Drew and Fry – who knew Nehru and Nkrumah personally, to the extent they were able to make domestic calls on both – worked in India on Chandigarh, India's most ambitious post-independence project. They also designed the National Museum in Accra, built for Ghana's 1957 Independence Day celebrations, and contributed to the port city of Tema. To limit the geographical scope of 'the Tropics' (itself a colonial definition), which covers some 40 percent of the earth's surface, this book focuses on India and Ghana, where Drew and Fry primarily practised, and not Brazil or Sri Lanka. However, rather than focusing exclusively on European actors, our research centres and celebrates the many local architects working alongside them who have been insufficiently recognized, rendered almost invisible in the archives.

These local practitioners, with their complicated relationship to the architectural legacy of colonialism, appropriated and adapted Tropical Modernism in service to their own nation-building ends. In India, architects such as Habib Rahman, Achyut Kanvinde, Balkrishna Doshi, Shivdatt Sharma, Jeet Malhotra and Eulie Chowdhury sought to create an Indian Modernism that avoided mimicking the International Style or resorting to historical pastiche but would create a new fusion of old and new for the future. In Africa, Theodore Shealtiel Clerk, John Owusu Addo, Victor Adegbite, Max Bond and Henry Wellington explored ways in which Tropical Modernism could be adapted to promote the excitement and possibilities of Nkrumah's Pan-African ideals. A few of these figures, now in their nineties, are still alive, and we had the honour of interviewing them for this project. All of them

Christmas card to Le Corbusier
by Fry and Drew sent from
Chandigarh, 1953

Four years before independence,
reflecting his growing
international fame, Nkrumah
appeared on the cover of *Time*,
9 February 1953

should be better known, recognized and celebrated for their great contribution to Modernism.

The South Kensington Museum, now the Victoria and Albert Museum, was opened by Queen Victoria in 1857, a month after the Indian Rebellion against the rule of the British East India Company, whose brutal suppression led to the formation of the British Raj. In 1879 the Company's collection of 20,000 objects was transferred to the V&A where it joined other imperial booty such as the Ashanti gold regalia plundered in the British 'punitive raid' on Kumasi, Ghana in 1874. The museum is now reckoning with this imperial past and its racial assumptions, with curators and others complicating and enriching the narratives of our 'global' museum. Deimperialization, as Kuan-Hsing Chen defines it, is 'the painful critical process where the colonizer examines the conduct, motives, desires, and the harmful consequences of imperial history on the world'.[7] The V&A's exploration of this subject is part of a wider and ongoing research project and partnership between the museum, the Architectural Association and Kwame Nkrumah University of Science and Technology – where the AA was invited by Nkrumah to establish an outpost in the 1960s – to investigate the shared cultural history and lessons of Tropical Modernism.

The story of Tropical Modernism is one of colonialism and decolonization, politics and power, defiance and independence. It is not just about the past, but also about the present and the future. Many of the buildings discussed, be they the contested heritage of colonialism or from the period of optimism after independence, are under threat of demolition or have already been destroyed. We hope that this project might provoke a reappraisal of their cultural value. As we face ecological challenges, there are also important lessons for the future in Tropical Modernism, an architecture that sought to be sustainable and to design with rather than against climate. India and Africa are particularly vulnerable to climate change and, as we look to a greener future, there is much we can learn more widely from Tropical Modernism's principles of climatic design and thermal comfort.

The Invention of Tropical Modernism

The African Experiment

(Previous spread) Student dormitories
at Mfantsipim School, Cape Coast by Fry,
Drew & Partners, 1953

Wesley Girls' School,
Cape Coast by Fry,
Drew & Partners, 1955

Mfantsipim School, Cape Coast
by Fry, Drew & Partners, 1953

Ola Uduku

Ola Uduku is Head of Liverpool School of Architecture. Her research specialisms are in modern architecture in West Africa and the history of educational architecture in Africa. She is co-lead of AHUWA, the Liverpool School of Architecture Research Centre focusing on architecture and urbanism in Western Africa, and is currently researching hospitals and healthcare architecture in Africa, and the architecture of aid.

Ghana's past, in terms of its governance, is tied to the heinous past of the slave trade, and the symbolism of its forts is linked to this past of slavery, colonization and domination. This context is very important to Tropical Modernism, which could be seen as an instrument of colonial power. The development of tropical-style Modernism in West Africa was very much on the back of what had already been a colonial architecture, because those involved in developing Tropical Modernism were operating as agents of the colonies at the time. West Africa became the perfect laboratory for experimenting with the International Style and adapting it to the requirements of the hot, humid climate of the Tropics.

For younger architects such as Maxwell Fry, Jane Drew and others, West Africa was an important place in which to develop, design and experiment. It was relatively close to Britain: you could board a mail boat in Liverpool or Southampton and be in Lagos or Accra in about 10 or 11 days. Fry was deployed in Ghana during the Second World War and stayed as a town-planning officer employed by the British Government; his wife, Jane Drew, followed him out there and they worked together. They were the colonists and had a very colonialist understanding of architecture in the Tropics, seeing very little value in the traditional building materials, methods and techniques of what I guess they deemed the 'primitive' society they were coming into.

What Fry and Drew were able to bring to the table, however, was their education and their understanding of climate through environmental science. Using these ideas, and by incorporating new materials such as concrete, they were able to make living in the Tropics more comfortable. The first beneficiaries of these experiments were English and European colonists, but the schools that were being developed and expanded as part of colonial policy at the time also gained by them. The colonists had a lot of interest in developing educational facilities in Africa; certainly, in West Africa, it seems to have been something that was both benevolent and felt to be strategically necessary.

Two good examples of Tropical Modernism in school design are Mfantsipim and Wesley Girls' School in Ghana. Both were originally small, missionary establishments but, with the investment of funds from the Colonial Development and Welfare Act, they were extended by Fry and Drew. What is characteristic of Tropical Modernism as it relates to schools is the long-school plan, with verandas, and importantly the use of brise soleils – useful both as a pattern for cutting out light and, by allowing for cross ventilation, for cooling the building. Such schools often also have an axial design, which in the case of Wesley Girls' makes the chapel the focus of the campus. From its colonial beginnings, we see here a Modernist interpretation of what a school might be in a tropical environment.

The Department of Tropical Architecture was formed after the Second World War at the Architectural Association (AA) in London. It was set up by Maxwell Fry, very much in association with Drew. It came about after a Nigerian architect called Adedokun Adeyemi – at the time a student at the University of Manchester – asked a question at a 1953 tropical architecture conference in London as to why African students were being taught about snow loads when they were not going to be dealing with snow back in Africa. There weren't many jobs in architecture in Britain at the time, and a whole raft of what I would call 'young Turks' were looking at designing elsewhere, particularly in Britain's colonial dependencies – places such as West Africa. The department taught students the new environmental science around how best to design in the Tropics.

After independence, Tropical Modernism was one of the tools by which Kwame Nkrumah was able to present his new Ghana to the world. While Ghana had obviously been a British colony (and most of its architects British), the politics changed in the post-independence era, as Nkrumah became involved with the Non-Aligned Movement and with socialism. Architects were being employed from Eastern Europe, Israel, Russia and even parts of China. African architects also became more prominent, because one of Nkrumah's ideas was the Africanization of professions. Practices working in Ghana were now legally required to have Ghanaian architects as the lead or principal architects; therefore, there was an increase in indigenous practitioners, people like John Owusu Addo, Victor Adegbite and Max Bond. And we should situate the architecture in the cultural moment of Africa at the time: really interesting creatives such as Chinua Achebe and Ama Ata Aidoo were producing fantastic literature; we had amazing textiles; there was highlife music. Africa was really finding its place in a world setting.

In 1963 the AA formed a partnership with the Kwame Nkrumah University of Science and Technology's architecture school. Its first head was John (Michael) Lloyd, who was sent from the AA to Ghana. Lloyd is an interesting character: he was half Norwegian, and it seems he brought this Scandinavian sensibility to his leadership style. If Fry and Drew were the young Turks of their day, Lloyd and his associates – effectively the generation later – were slightly hippy, different in their attitude to architecture. Lloyd encouraged students to appreciate their context. It was part of their course to go into the regions and do community projects, meaning that traditional forms and practices of architecture in Africa became part of a curriculum for the first time.

Nkrumah's downfall in 1966 sounded the death knell for Tropical Modernism as a style and as a concept. It coincided with the collapse of a lot of African economies: in Ghana, the collapse in cocoa prices effectively bankrupted the country. But some of the ideas of Tropical Modernism remain really, really important in how we think about what a future African architecture might be. It's again going to be very important, for instance, to design with climate in mind. Given the different requirements of buildings today from those of the 1960s and '70s, how can we make the Tropics another laboratory for future experiments around living in the 21st century?

National Museum, Accra by
Fry, Drew, Drake and Lasdun, 1957

Chapter

(Opposite) Members of the Gold Coast Regiment protecting Elmina Castle, built by the Portuguese in 1482 as a trading post for gold and slaves, 1930s

A durbar in Gold Coast, watched by British colonials in pith helmets, 1930s

In 1944 British architect Jane Drew went to Baker's, the tropical outfitters in London's Golden Square, to be fitted for mosquito boots and a pith helmet. As she tried on long gloves, she gazed at the numerous photos of slain tigers and elephants that decorated the walls. She was buying protection for her trip to West Africa, a place once known as the 'white man's grave' because of deadly tropical diseases such as malaria, which were now treatable.[1] A few days later she boarded a boat from Liverpool to Tokoradi on the Gold Coast (now Ghana), travelling with the traders, colonials and missionaries who made up the white cast of colonial West Africa. 'I remember when I first saw the dark shape of Africa how hopeless it looked,' Drew recalled of the view from her ship in an unpublished memoir: 'its dirty green and swampy moth-eaten fetid air.'[2]

There were 50 slave forts along the Gold Coast, built by the Portuguese, Dutch and British, through which many of the almost 13 million enslaved Africans passed as they were sold, branded and shipped to the New World. At Fort Christiansborg (now called Osu Castle) in Accra, before the trade was abolished in 1807, slaves were kept in airless, stinking cellars below those used to store alcohol. The British Governor-General of the Gold Coast lived above, attending church and supervising proceedings in tiled rooms with breezy views over the Gulf of Guinea and miles of golden beach. Enslaved Africans would have been led from the castle's dungeon down a long, damp passage and through the 'Door of No Return'; the sandy beach is the last bit of Africa over which, blinded by the light, they would have walked before being ferried to transport ships. Once aboard they were kept in even worse conditions than at the forts. Fifteen percent would not survive the transatlantic crossing.

On arrival in Tokoradi after 10 days at sea, Drew and her baggage were lowered in a basket into finely decorated surf boats and paddled to shore where she boarded a bus to Accra. The journey was, she said,

> [an] awful shock ... I was simply unprepared for the mud villages in a state of shocking disrepair and corrugated or thatch but very rough roofs, nor for the people

wearing cotton vests with holes in them everywhere. I don't know what I had thought I would meet, but the reality was hard to take. Africans were jammed utterly tight and overflowing into their lorries and it was terribly hot and sticky. The sight of the awful swampy land and the eroded village streets. I got no feeling of the noble savage but poor slum dwellers in slums worse than I had imagined.[3]

While studying at the Architecture Association (AA) in London 13 years earlier, Drew had appeared in the AA Christmas pantomime as one such 'noble savage', wearing a grass skirt and black face, and she still had these racial prejudices about Africa and Britain's 'civilizing' role there. 'We were brought up to believe we were superior to everyone else,' Drew later recalled.[4] At the panto, after some jokes about Modernism and its rejection in Britain – 'Who is Corbusier, what is he / That Englishmen ignore him / Round the corner, under a tree / Hide the soil pipe of your W.C.' – there was, according to the AA's student reviewer, 'some more Outposts of Empire stuff, and in British Goods our patriotism was once more stirred by noble feelings nobly presented'.[5] Of Drew's character, the review adds: 'I still wonder how long it took Amami to get her make-up off.'[6]

Drew was one of Britain's first Modernist architects. She set up an all-female practice in 1939, and at the time she travelled to West Africa to join her husband, Maxwell Fry, she had recently curated an exhibition, *Rebuilding Britain* (1943), at the National Gallery. Fry, 12 years Drew's senior, had enlisted in the Royal Engineers in the Second World War and been stationed in the Gold Coast, which he dismissed as 'some place where soldiers wear pith helmets and very wide, overlength shorts'; he was responsible, amongst other things, for maintaining the country's old forts.[7] Drew and Fry had been married on 25 April 1942 – Fry's final day in Britain. 'We were photographed outside [Caxton Hall, Westminster] on the pavement', Fry recalled. 'Jane in a ravishing hat looking quizzically at her victim, his trousers still not as military as they should be, but he smiling with insane satisfaction and relief.'[8] Before he signed up, the pair had been working with fellow

MARS Group New Architecture
Exhibition, 1938;
poster designed by
Edward McKnight Kauffer

(Opposite) Impington Village
College, Cambridge by Fry and
Gropius, 1938

66 Old Church Street, Chelsea,
London by Fry
and Gropius, 1938

Letter from Fry to Drew depicting
him at work in West Africa, 1944

members of the avant-garde Modern Architectural Research Group (MARS) on the London plan, a radical proposal to reimagine the bombed out capital as a post-war Modernist city, with bacon-like strips of ordered development neatly arranged around the meandering spine of the Thames.

Drew and Fry formed an architectural as well as life partnership, embracing a utopian ideal that hoped a radical new architecture in concrete, glass and steel would build a better world. Modernism had developed in Europe in the 1920s with the Swiss-born French architect Le Corbusier and the German founder of the Bauhaus art school Walter Gropius its leading advocates; they were the founding members of the Congrès Internationaux d'Architecture Moderne (CIAM), established in 1928, of which Fry and Drew were members and MARS, the small coterie of architects and critics that they helped form, the British chapter. Their revolutionary architecture placed the function of the building at the heart of its design, with clean lines, unornamented façades, expanses of glass and flat roofs. However, Fry and Drew were working against the grain: this minimalist aesthetic, with its explicit rejection of tradition, failed to take root in Britain where it was seen as too severe for British tastes. The painter Wyndham Lewis described Modernism as 'cod-liver oil to the sweet Anglo-Saxon palette'.[9]

In 1934, having fled to London to escape Nazi persecution, Gropius formed an architectural partnership with Fry. Because Modernism was initially unpopular in Britain, their collaboration only produced Impington Village College in Cambridgeshire and two sleek luxury villas, including 66 Old Church Street in Chelsea. Gropius left for America in 1937, complaining that England was an 'inartistic country'.[10] After a farewell dinner at the Isokon Building in Hampstead – where Gropius lived in a rare Modernist apartment block intended as an experiment in futuristic and communal living – he invited Fry to come with him. Fry refused; instead, he and Drew looked for opportunities in colonial West Africa, where they found a more hospitable environment than Britain and developed Tropical Modernism. As the architectural historian Mark Crinson writes, Modernism, imagined as a type of benevolent technical expertise, arrived in Africa 'less in triumph than retreat'.[11]

Letter from Fry to Drew featuring
designs for University College
Ibadan, Nigeria, 1954

Wastepaper basket Fry designed
in West Africa for his own use,
*c.*1945

In 1944 Fry had been appointed an advisor on planning to Lord Swinton, Resident Minister in the four West African colonies (Gambia, the Gold Coast, Nigeria and Sierra Leone); he accepted on condition that Drew could join him as his assistant. Having last worked together on the London Plan, they would mastermind rehousing, slum clearance and town-planning schemes in West Africa. Fry had warned her of the Tropics: 'The heat is intolerable, heat and humidity ... it is the humidity that is making life so hard to bear at the moment. I am damned moist and unpleasant and the brain barely ticks over.' He added: 'Mosquitoes apply themselves to their gift.'[12] On arrival in West Africa, Fry, like other colonial officials, would have been given a copy of the *Gold Coast Handbook* (1937), a government publication propagating the view that it was the imperial duty to slowly prepare a backward West Africa for democratic self-government. Fry shared this colonial prejudice, writing to Drew in October 1944 that it would be their role to give Africans 'courage and a belief in their future, for I think the English have a grand job to do for the world. Never grander than at this time, even if it is the last and final grandeur'.[13]

Fry lived in what he described as 'an expatriate paradise of bungalows buried in vegetation'.[14] This white enclave was separated from the African populations by a *cordon sanitaire*, a 'building free zone' ('four forty yards between Europeans and Africans') designed to prevent the perceived threat of transmission of disease.[15] Like a Modernist bowerbird, Fry had decorated his one-storey house with furniture of his own design: 'Bauhaus table lamps done in mahogany, huge basket globe pendants, trays in plaited grasses, bowls with Paul Klee designs by potters who had never heard of him. Curtains of Hausa cloth, the most elegant and aristocratic cheetah rugs ... The total effect when installed was like a dolls house set piece and delighted Jane.'[16] The V&A holds a wastepaper basket that Fry designed for himself at this time, decorated with a pierced pattern similar to those he later used in the decorative façades of his West African buildings.

Drew did indeed acknowledge that it looked like 'a New York Penthouse ... but it was hot, damp, and the journey had been utterly depressing' and she arrived in a terrible mood. The couple went to the segregated seafront European Club – known to its members simply as 'The Club' – where white colonials looked out over the sea and drank waves of anti-malarial pink gin, which helped cheer her up (Fry had won someone else's Black cook there in a game of poker). 'English people behaved different in Africa,' she noted; they were 'caricatures of their original selves'.[17]

Their office was a shingle-roofed hut with doors and windows open on each side to mitigate the heat by letting the fresh and dry trade winds blow through it – a technique from which Fry and Drew would learn when building their own Tropical Modernist buildings. From one window, as Fry described it, you could see the 'scrubby grass of the "building free zone", once golf course, with colonial buildings, palms, a union jack flying over the clubhouse, the complete Noel Coward background. From the other, in blinding light, a line of pounding surf.'[18] With no formally qualified West African architects then available, Fry and Drew began to train a small African staff of six, Fry grumbling that 'to introduce the art of town planning to West Africa was a far-fetched proposition equivalent to teaching 12-tone music to a village choir'.[19]

They tested out their city plans in a series of exhibitions to which, at Drew's instigation, they invited local chiefs to consult: 'with great beating of drums and in full ceremonials of parasol, wands and insignia of office, they presented themselves', wrote Fry.[20] The pair had prepared large, coloured relief plans to show their ideas to reform Accra but discovered that the Africans wanted concrete houses, like the Europeans, which used an expensive imported material, rather than the rammed earth ones proposed. Drew, who Gropius described as devouring life with a 'fork and a spoon', often overrode conventions and operated, as her husband admitted, with 'careless indifference to feelings' (one commissioner said that Drew was 'not *persona grata* in certain quarters of West Africa').[21] The couple had very different but complementary personalities: extrovert and introvert, they were united in a shared belief that architecture could improve the world. 'The strength of her nature was to be outgoing and immediate,' wrote Fry, 'mine for longer objectives, but no less tenacious. She was warm and baroque. I was cooler, more contemplative, less

open, but determined. Each of us dreamed our dreams and they often co-mingled.'[22]

★

As the war was coming to an end, Sir James Gurney, then Acting Governor of the Gold Coast, told Fry and Drew that the Colonial and Development and Welfare Fund had dedicated £200m (equivalent to £6 billion today) to 'good causes, and we are determined to start a big school building programme at once. Of course, we could send for some big-wig architect from London, but here are you nice creatures, deep in the country and loving it. Why shouldn't it be you?'[23] The money for reforming, rebuilding and modernizing Britain's colonies was intended both to offset growing calls for independence by showing Britain's good and generous government, and to stimulate economic growth and promote trade with the imperial centre by educating a new administrative middle class. Unable to find interesting work in London, Fry and Drew leapt at the chance to be the first to benefit from the 'big spending era', as Fry described it, and set up offices in Accra and Lagos.[24] West Africa became an experimental laboratory for British architects, providing opportunities to test and explore ideas in commissions and operational freedoms they would not have had at home.

'When we went to West Africa there seemed to be no indigenous architecture,' recalled Drew. 'We therefore tried to invent an architecture which specifically met the needs of the West Africans and dealt with climate and the diseases it brought with it.'[25] Fry decreed more bluntly that there was 'nothing to be learned from traditional African architecture'. (This reflected a long-standing prejudice: in Banister Fletcher's 1905 'Tree of Architecture', Sub-Saharan Africa is not included.) 'We looked around for architectural precedent but there was none', wrote Fry:

Not in our own colonial building which was without character or the sort of response to the natural conditions we were engaged upon. Not in African building which though it taught us the value of shade, was of a different and a passing order, the beauty of which we could admire as it fell decayed before the onslaught of

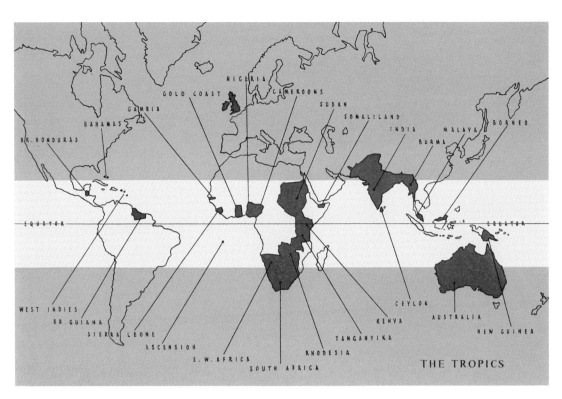

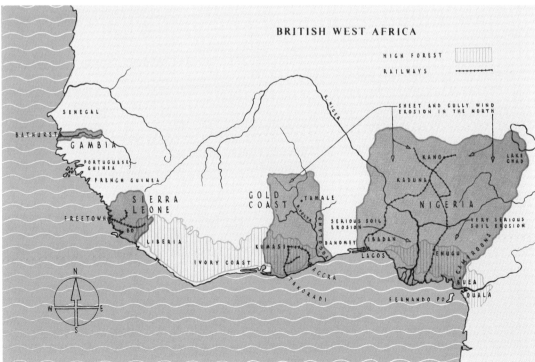

'The Tropics' and four West African countries then under British colonial rule, from *Village Housing in the Tropics* by Drew and Fry, 1947

35

Gordon Cullen's illustration
for the 1953 issue
of *The Architectural
Review* featuring Fry and
Drew's West African projects

the West. We were fated to make new architecture out of love for the place and obedience to nature, and to make it with cement and steel, asbestos sheets, wood above the termite line, glass, and not much else.[26]

They brought with them what Fry described as 'a new apparatus of thought', learned from CIAM and the MARS group, and believed their own technological solutions to climate issues superior to the local ones that had been developed over centuries.[27] Fry and Drew used the latest environmental and building science to adapt Modernism, originally designed for Europe's temperate climate, to the hot and humid conditions of the Tropics, with its heavier rainfall. They defined this geographical zone in their book, *Village Housing in the Tropics* (1947), a pocket guide to self-building in hot climates ('a charmingly dated account of both a Westerner's view of the architecture, and the social anthropology of life among the "natives" in the tropics', according to architectural historian Ola Uduku).[28] The Tropics – a broad strip running 0°–15° north and south of the equator, covering 40 percent of the world's surface – was a colonial definition that encompassed most of the territories of the British Empire but ignored regional variations in climate, altitude and population as well as cultures and traditions.

To 'invent' Tropical Modernism, Fry and Drew made full use of the newest climate research and building techniques. The research station they designed in Kumasi to collect information on climate and the suitability of local building materials and technologies was essentially a field office of the Tropical Building Section of the Building Research Station in Watford, north-west of London (which disseminated data around the Empire in a series of Colonial Building Notes). Analysing solar-path movements and meteorological data, Fry and Drew developed principles that would provide passive cooling. To design against the heat, they orientated buildings east-west, so that the sun travelled over the spines of their roofs, which had double skins to absorb the heat and wide eaves to provide shade. This was a practical deviation from the flat-roofed forms of European Modernism; their later buildings would have monopitch roofs. Buildings were long and often only one room deep so that they could be effectively

Village Housing in the Tropics
by Drew and Fry, 1947

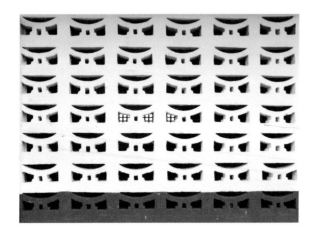

Brise soleil at Opoku Ware School, Kumasi, 1953–5, based on the design of an Ashanti stool

cross-ventilated, while brise soleils, or perforated screens, and adjustable louvres allowed in a cooling breeze.

In May 1953 the magazine *Architectural Review* published Fry and Drew's various West African projects as a single body of work for the first time. Entitled 'African Experiment', the article was accompanied by an illustration by Gordon Cullen of an unidentified Fry and Drew African school with emphatic brise soleils and, in a gesture of paternalism, a Black child in silhouette (a common trope in the photography of these buildings). The *Architectural Review* explored their work at Mfantsipim, Adisadel and Wesley in Cape Coast where they built enormous new school campuses or created Modernist extensions to missionary institutions. It was at such institutions, which reinforced western systems of knowledge, opinions and morals, that a new generation of administrators and specialists was to be trained. Often these designs, with their elongated plans, were focused on a bell and water tower, a traditional symbol of Christian power and colonial occupation.

To ornament the rhythmic façades of their buildings, Fry and Drew made superficial reference to West African motifs, such as the Adinkra symbols that appear on textiles and other crafts, which they described as 'relics of this beautiful savage life'.[29] African art played a key role in the development of a Modernist aesthetic in the early twentieth century. European artists such as Picasso and Paolozzi exoticized and appropriated the sculptural abstraction they admired in artefacts of colonial conquest encountered in ethnographic museums, where they were stripped of their ritual significance. The African patterns that Fry and Drew use in their distinctive brise soleils were similarly primitivist and add, as the architecture critic Nikolaus Pevsner noted, 'an element of fantasy' that corroded the International Style's strict rules against ornament.[30] This concession to the locality is seen at Opuku Ware School in the Ashanti heartland of Kumasi, where the profile of an Ashanti stool, a sacred symbol of chiefly power, is repeated in a brise soleil to create a distinctive pattern that would have been immediately recognizable to local students.

Fry and Drew considered University College Ibadan, Nigeria, built between 1949 and 1960, to be the best illustration of their theories and techniques. The long façade of its library has an

Diagram of a brise soleil at Aburi Girls'
School from *Tropical Architecture in the
Humid Zone* by Drew and Fry, 1956

Student leaning against brise soleil at
University College Ibadan, 1962

Campus designs by Fry and Drew in West Africa, 1946-55. Clockwise from top right: University College Ibadan, Adisadel Teacher Training College, University College Ibadan, Aburi Girls' School. Opposite: University College Ibadan.

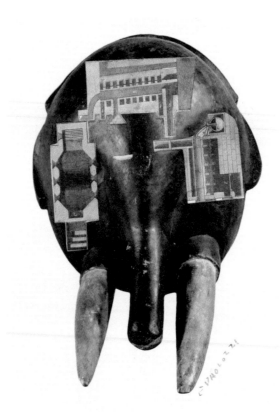

Collage featuring a Congolese elephant mask by Eduardo Paolozzi who taught alongside Fry and Drew at the Department of Tropical Architecture, 1946–7

almost lace-like brise soleil whose pattern is reminiscent of the mud-brick mosques in West Africa, and it appeared on the cover of both the March 1961 issue of *The West African Builder and Architect*, which was edited by Robert Atkinson, a staffer from their Nigerian office, and May 1955's *Architectural Design*, where a figure in Nigerian Hausa dress is superimposed over the grille pattern to emphasize the textile quality of the skin of the building. Their decorative Tropical Modernism – cool, white, pristine constructions seemingly grounded in climate-responsive science – attracted a great deal of international attention in the architectural press and glossy magazines.

Fry and Drew were the acknowledged leaders in the field, and certainly the best self-publicists, but they weren't the only practitioners of Tropical Modernism. Other architects, such as Kenneth 'Winky' Scott, Leo de Syllas and James Cubitt – all of whom had affiliations to the AA and had been stationed in the region when in the British Army – set up their own practices in West Africa and practised in this style. They all took advantage of the new opportunities provided by the rapid development there, facilitated by the Colonial Development and Welfare Act. 'Architectural prejudices are less seriously entrenched in Nigeria than in England,' wrote De Syllas of the Architects' Co-Partnership, who moved their office to Lagos in the 1950s for lack of work in Britain, later claiming to have only once in three years had a building refused in Nigeria for being 'too modern'.[31] In 1956 Cubitt designed a doll's house for Princess Anne, a miniature version of the Library Board Bungalow he had built for the chief librarian in Accra, but it was unlikely he would have been able to build Modernism at scale back home.

British architects working in West Africa relied on a local workforce that has long remained unrecognized, and which goes unmentioned in most books about Fry and Drew. In photographs of these Black architects with Drew and Fry in the RIBA archive they are labelled in the catalogue merely as 'African assistants'. The contribution of this pioneering generation of architects, who assumed important roles post-independence, is only now being properly acknowledged. It includes figures like Theodore Shealtiel Clerk, who trained at the University of Edinburgh and returned

March 1961 issue of *The West African Builder and Architect* no. 1 featuring University College Ibadan

May 1955 cover of *Architectural Design* depicting a Nigerian man in Hausa dress overlaid with a brise soleil from University College Ibadan

Clockwise from top right:
Fry and Drew with their Accra office,
including Theodore Shealtiel Clerk and
Peter Turkson, 1942; Fry with Theo
Crosby and John Noah, 1940s; Fry with
Harry L. Ford and Theodore Shealtiel
Clerk, 1943

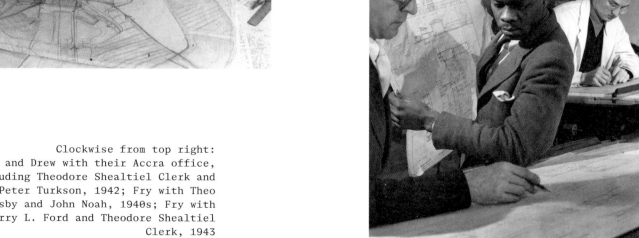

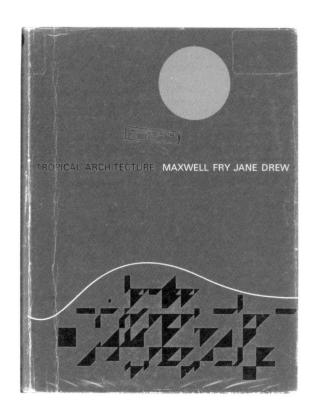

Tropical Architecture in the Dry and Humid Zones by Drew and Fry, 1964 (an updated version of the original 1956 book)

to the Gold Coast as the first professionally qualified Ghanaian architect in 1946, working for Fry and Drew before Ghana gained independence, and Peter Turkson, who worked for the couple before leaving the Gold Coast in 1949 to pursue his studies at the University of Liverpool, then returned to Ghana in 1956 to become the first Ghanaian chief physical-planning officer in 1961. Fry and Drew also employed West Africans in their London office, including John Noah from Sierra Leone – a fact that they used to their advantage when seeking commissions there.

Fry and Drew were also instrumental in the formation of the Department of Tropical Architecture, or Tropical School, launched in 1954 at the Architectural Association (AA) in London. The School was founded following the recommendation of a 1953 tropical architecture conference attended by 400 people, where the Nigerian student Adedokun Adeyemi, who had helped organize the conference, complained that while he was learning a lot about fireplaces and snow loads, his university training was an inadequate preparation for work when he returned home to Nigeria. Fry – back in London after three years spent building the Modernist city of Chandigarh in India with Le Corbusier – was offered the job as the School's first director, accepting with 'alacrity' according to the German-Jewish émigré Otto Koenigsberger who co-founded the department with Fry and Leo de Syllas. Given Fry's prestige, his hiring was considered something of a coup by the AA.[32] The department had 20 students, almost all from the UK, who were to be trained in the principles of climatic design and thermal comfort, ready for work in Britain's colonies.

Fry and Drew's book *Tropical Architecture in the Humid Zone* (1956) became a key textbook for the course, but the buildings featured are largely by British architects, and no African architects are included (a second edition in 1964 would include Balkrishna Doshi and Geoffrey Bawa as the only South Asian representatives). However, the year it was published, student numbers had dwindled to six and Fry, distracted by several important commissions including continuing work at the University of Ibadan, recommended the closure of the school. In 1957 Otto Koenigsberger took over as director and the student body rose to 40, almost all from the newly independent countries of the British

Nigerian student Vivian Uku
receives his diploma from
the Department of Tropical
Architecture, 1963

A studio at the Architecture
Association, 1960s

Commonwealth. Koenigsberger had been working not far from the AA, at the School of Medicine and Tropical Hygiene, where he was researching the effects of climate on housing design (the origins of his 1974 book *Manual of Tropical Housing and Building*); he had served as Director of Housing in post-Partition India and worked in Ghana as planning advisor on the Volta River Project and on the first United Nations housing mission to the country.

The Department of Tropical Architecture, in propagating and exporting Tropical Modernism as a style, had a global impact and its alumni formed an influential network of practitioners working in the tropical zone. The Department taught students that, by applying environmental and building science as well as modern technology, Tropical Modernism was superior to vernacular build-ings, from which there was little to learn. The curriculum had a western bias that reflected the late colonial origins of Tropical Modernism and its universalist, centralized approach failed to address the varying cultures and conditions of the vast and different 'tropical zone'.

As critics such as Hannah le Roux and Ola Uduku have made clear, Tropical Modernism sought to create conditions of 'comfort', defined in western terms, to make working conditions easier for colonial administrators as well as those that they sought to exploit and render more productive. The alliance with the School of Medicine and Tropical Hygiene, established to train doctors to treat Britain's colonial administrators and work in its tropical empire, was not accidental; Drew's father was a doctor and, as she put it, 'saw everything from a hygiene point of view', which carried through to Tropical Modernism's controlled and suppos-edly purifying use of sanitizing light and air.[33]

★

Fry and Drew's Tropical Modernism, a late imperial architecture, developed against the backdrop of political unrest and decolonial struggle, which would soon come to fruition. After the Second World War, many colonies wanted recognition for their contribu-tion to the war effort by being granted independence: almost a third of the world's population then lived under colonial rule. Calls for self-government had been mounting for decades, including in West Africa where the 65,000-strong Gold Coast Regiment had

Otto Koenigsberger with students
at the Department of Tropical
Architecture, *c.*1958

view of a courtyard

view of a shopping street

ARCHITECTURAL ASSOCIATION
SCHOOL OF ARCHITECTURE
STORE
148   YEAR   1954-55

onitsha   market   nigeria
d. lakofski   r. scott brown.

OM 3

Design project for a
market in Onitsha, Nigeria
by Denise Lakofski (Scott
Brown) and Robert Scott
Brown, 1954–5

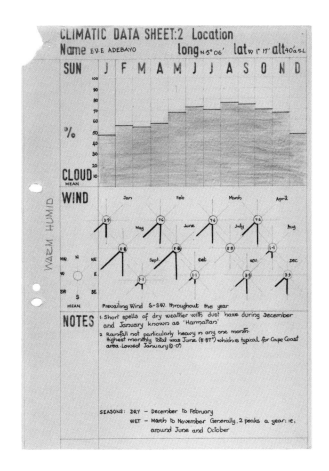

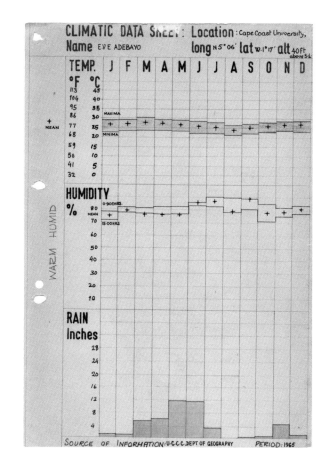

Climatic data calculations
for a project at Cape Coast
University by
E.V.E. Adebayo, 1965

The curriculum for
the Department of Tropical
Architecture, 1964–5

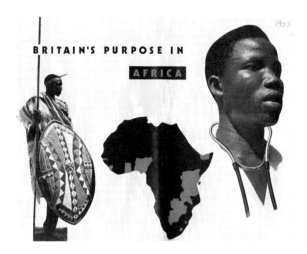

(Opposite) The 5th Pan-African
Congress in Manchester,
photographed by John Deakin, 1945

Britain's Purpose in Africa,
British Information Services, 1955

The logo of the Pan-African
Federation, 1940s

seen combat in North Africa and elsewhere in the Commonwealth and wanted to be rewarded for these efforts. The Atlantic Charter of 1941 created a vision for a post-war world in which there was restoration of self-government for victims of Nazism, and self-determination for other countries that wanted democracy and freedom. However, while Germany was fighting to create an empire, the British were fighting to maintain one and, under Winston Churchill, the UK still advocated a policy of gradualism, deeming their colonies not yet ready for independence.

The writer, filmmaker and art historian Nana Oforiatta Ayim makes clear that imperialists were always unwelcome in Africa and that the drive to self-rule in the Gold Coast began the year after the British colony was formed in 1868, when the Fante Confederacy demanded self-government. After the Second World War, a leading figure in this story of opposition was Kwame Nkrumah, a Gold Coast student who had been radicalized by Mussolini's invasion of Ethiopia, news of which he heard about when in London in 1935. 'At that moment', he wrote, 'it was almost as if the whole of London had declared war on me personally. For the next few minutes I could do nothing but glare at each impassive face wondering if these people could possibly realise the wickedness of colonialism … My nationalism surged to the fore.'[34] In his 1936 book *How Britain Rules Africa*, the American intellectual and Pan-Africanist George Padmore, whose father had been born into slavery in Barbados and who would become Nkrumah's mentor, called all forms of imperial domination 'colonial fascism'. 'Colonies are the breeding ground for the type of fascist mentality which is being let loose in Europe today,' he wrote. 'The fight against fascism cannot be separated from the right of all colonial peoples and subject races to Self-Determination.'[35]

Since the 1900 Pan-African Congress in London, political leaders and intellectuals from Europe, North America and Africa had gathered to discuss strategies to end colonial rule and racial discrimination. After the 'scramble for Africa' in the late nineteenth century, these Congresses solidified anti-colonial resistance and solidarity between Africa and its diaspora, linked by the common experience of oppression and slavery, colonialism and racism. As Priyamvada Gopal points out, it was easier to articulate criticism

Nkrumah's release from
Fort James prison, 1951

Demonstration in Trafalgar Square,
London against the handling of the
Gold Coast riots, 1948

of the Empire in the Metropolis, with its active Black press, than in Britain's colonies where opposition was subject to repressive anti-sedition legislation. Though the slave trade was abolished in 1807 (and slavery in 1833), Pan-African intellectuals including W.E.B. Du Bois, C.L.R. James, Padmore and Nkrumah all made explicit connections between slavery and colonialism, in terms of capitalist exploitation and the disenfranchisement of Africans. In making those connections, and because of the involuntary contribution of enslaved peoples, they also argued for Africa's role to be recognized in the co-production of modernity.

In 1945, just weeks after the armistice, the 5th Pan-African Congress was held at Chorlton-on-Medlock Town Hall in Manchester. Du Bois, the 'Father of Pan-Africanism', was honorary president and Nkrumah was one of the organizers, as was Jomo Kenyatta, the future president of Kenya. Addressing the hall of 200 delegates, Nkrumah argued that 'full and unconditional Independence' was the only goal for Africa's colonies, even if revolutionary methods were required to achieve it. *Picture Post* was one of the few media outlets to report on the event, sending the former war journalist Hilde Marchant and photographer John Deakin (famed for his alcohol-drenched images of Soho) to cover it. Deakin's photos show the hall decorated with posters bearing the slogans 'Africa for the Africans', 'Freedom for all subject people', 'Oppressed Peoples of the World Unite', 'Freedom of the press in the colonies!' and 'Arabs and Jews Unite against British Imperialism'.[36] Du Bois remarked that the Congress made 1945 'a decisive year in determining the freedom of Africa' by laying the groundwork for independence.[37] Nkrumah, who became general secretary of the working committee established to take things forward, similarly remembered the 5th Congress as a turning point, saying 'we went from Manchester knowing definitely where we were going'.[38]

India won independence in 1947 after a long campaign of civil disobedience by anti-colonial activists including Mahatma Gandhi and Jawaharlal Nehru, whose books Nkrumah read as a student. The peaceful campaigns of their Swadeshi movement not only helped India achieve independence but influenced non-violent freedom movements across the world. An important turning point

The British colonial secretariat,
Gold Coast, 1947

Governor Arden-Clarke, Nkrumah
and the first all-African
cabinet, 1952

in India's struggle for independence was the Salt March of 1930, when Gandhi led a 24-day, 241-mile walk to protest a tax on salt levied on the Indian people by the British government. In response, Britain arrested over 60,000 peaceful protesters, including Gandhi and Nehru, which only served to increase support for home rule in India. The year of India's independence, Kwame Nkrumah returned to the Gold Coast from London, where he had studied philosophy at University College under A.J. Ayer ('It was a way of marking time until the opportunity came for him to return to Ghana', Ayer said of his poor student), and implemented a campaign of 'Positive Action' inspired by their success.[39]

After 12 years abroad, Nkrumah, as Secretary of the United Gold Coast Convention (UGCC), the Gold Coast's first indigenous political party, proved a skilful political operator. He implemented a campaign of non-violent political protests, strikes and boycotts inspired by Gandhi and Nehru's work in India. This culminated in the 1948 riots that started in Accra after a crowd of unarmed war veterans marched in protest on Osu Castle, where the colonial Governor lived, hoping to deliver a petition; they were shot at by colonial troops, who killed three of the marchers and wounded several others. This sparked five days of rioting, which spread to Adisadel School in Cape Coast (designed by Drew and Fry), with rioters later being expelled, to Kumasi and elsewhere. Nkrumah and the other so-called 'Big 6' who led the UGCC were accused of inciting the violence and were imprisoned by the British in the Northern Territories.

On his release, Nkrumah founded the Convention People's Party (CPP), which was even more radical than the UGCC and held mass rallies with the popular slogan 'Self-government NOW!' He was imprisoned again in 1950 for organizing a general strike which also turned violent – but, fearful of communist revolution, the British agreed to democratic elections. With Nkrumah campaigning from prison, the CPP won 34 of the 38 available seats in the 1951 Gold Coast general election; Nkrumah, who had been elected to the Accra constituency, was released and became the Leader of Government Business with responsibility for running the Gold Coast alongside Governor Sir Charles Noble Arden-Clarke in all matters apart from defence and foreign affairs. He was the

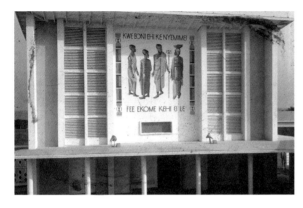

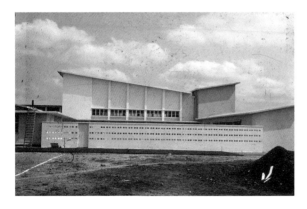

Community Centre, Accra by Fry and
Drew, 1951, funded by the
United Africa Company in response
to Accra riots, with mural by
Kofi Antubam

Gold Coast's de facto first prime minister, leading an all-African cabinet – an important first step towards Ghanaian independence, for which he continued to campaign. In a new position of authority, and describing Ghanaians as still 'half slaves and half free', Nkrumah now sought independence through constitutional means.[40]

The Community Centre that Fry and Drew designed for Accra in 1951 was funded by the British-owned United Africa Company – an attempt to restore the company's reputation after their Accra headquarters was burned down in the 1948 riots in retaliation for their presumed price fixing. The building, which comprised an assembly hall surrounded by two courtyards, was used for concerts, plays and other public events. The central elevation features a mural by Ghanaian artist Kofi Antubam, who had trained at Goldsmiths' College in London and was head of the Art Department at Achimota College. Antubam cofounded the Sankofa Movement, named after an Akan word which means to retrieve from the past: 'I want to paint the actual, real life of my people,' he stated.[41] His mural, which offers 'reassuring images of pre-colonial rural life and a unified nation' according to Mark Crinson, features a stylized painting of three men looking at a woman who carries a basket on her head and a propagandistic phrase in the local Ga language: 'It is good we live together as friends and one people.'[42]

In 1955 British Information Services published a self-justifying leaflet, *Britain's Purpose in Africa,* which promoted the idea of gradualism and warned condescendingly that the belief that 'self-government is better than good government is a most dangerous half-truth'.[43] However, this cautionary note was sounded too late: the African Revolution was already underway. Ghana gained independence in 1957 and Antubam became Nkrumah's official state artist, designing the flag and symbols of the newly independent country, including the presidential seat, sword and mace. Over the next decade, two-thirds of the countries in Africa would win freedom from colonial power as the 'winds of change' blew across the continent.[44]

Community Centre, Accra by Fry
and Drew, 1951, with mural
by Kofi Antubam

Samia Nkrumah

Samia Nkrumah is a Ghanaian politician and, as the former chairperson of the Convention People's Party (CPP), was the first woman to head a major political party in Ghana. She is the only daughter of Ghana's first president, Kwame Nkrumah, and his Egyptian wife, Fathia Halim Rizk, and is the Founder and President of the Kwame Nkrumah Pan-African Centre (KNAC), an organization, set up to promote Kwame Nkrumah's vision, philosophy and political culture within the context of a united Africa.

Our father worked with many people of African descent when he was living in the States and in the UK, and one of those who had a great influence on his thinking was George Padmore, the great Trinidadian Pan-Africanist. Together they worked to set up the 1945 Pan-African Congress in Manchester, which was really a game-changer in African politics. It shaped the independence struggle and marked the beginning of decolonization on African soil.

Padmore and Nkrumah brought the whole decolonization struggle into focus, linking it with Black people's wider fight for justice. It was bigger than just attaining independence; it was about regaining our dignity, our sense of purpose in the world. Political independence was not separate from unity – the unity of all Africans everywhere, not just on the continent. Hence Kwame Nkrumah's famous statement that 'the independence of Ghana is meaningless unless it is linked up with the total liberation of Africa'. Independence and unity were his lifework, his vision.

A couple of years later, Nkrumah returned to the Gold Coast to join the nationalist independence movement at the time, and became the catalyst for our independence. He introduced Positive Action, an anti-colonial campaign of non-violence that contributed to our independence, which he wrote was influenced by India's independence struggle. The movement's agitation and protests culminated in the 1948 riots. As the General Secretary of the United Gold Coast Convention, our father was really in the middle of the action and was imprisoned. Elections were called; campaigning from prison, he won the most seats, and the colonial power had no option but to declare him leader of government business. So, in 1951, there was some kind of a power-sharing arrangement with the British colonial power.

To those who say Kwame Nkrumah was too radical, I always respond that history belies that, because he was actually fairly pragmatic. He spent the next six years trying to work out how to constitutionally attain independence and finally, in 1957, it became obvious that Ghanaians were ready for political independence, and for economic and social independence, which is what we were truly, truly hungry for. We all know that Ghana was the first Sub-Saharan country to liberate itself from colonialism. But without that Pan-Africanist vision, I don't think we would have gained independence when we did.

Ghana became independent in March 1957 and, at the end of that year, our father got married. We always used to tease our mother because it was an arranged marriage, a Pan-African political marriage: our father had sent emissaries to Cairo to look for a suitable bride. Egypt, which was free by the time Ghana gained independence, had helped us in our liberation struggle, and our father wanted to bring North Africa closer to the rest of the continent. A meeting was arranged in Accra with the help of Gamal Abdel Nasser, the president of Egypt; without his intervention, there was no way her family would have allowed their daughter to leave the country to come and meet this man with whom she didn't share a language. The moment she saw him, she thought: 'This is a very charming man.' And they got married there and then, the same day they met.

The unity of Ghana was something very important for our father and his vision. Because we were not one unit before independence, the Gold Coast had different territories. You had the Northern Territories, the Ashanti, and then Accra and the central region, Volta and Togoland, which joined us after a plebiscite. So, one of the things that our father was very concerned about was maintaining the unity and cohesion of this new nation. He endeavoured to resist tribalism and ethnic politics, and the National Museum he commissioned from Maxwell Fry and Jane Drew is a reflection of that. It's a way of saying that we've always lived in diversity – not just Ghana, but the whole continent – but that diversity does not mean disunity.

Nation-building after independence entailed a lot of construction, especially in education which, alongside manufacturing, was a major thrust of Kwame Nkrumah's domestic policy. A lot of schools were built, a lot of hospitals. It was a people-centred approach; Nkrumah had socialist leanings and a vision of uplifting the country from poverty. His attempts to impose his development aspirations brought him into conflict with some powerful forces, which put him at great risk – there were several attempts on his life. To help achieve his goals, he made Ghana a one-party state, which was not uncommon in Africa at the time. But by no stretch of the imagination would it be at all accurate to label a great leader like Kwame Nkrumah as a dictator without putting things in context.

In 1966 his government was overthrown, with help from the US government. The storm had been gathering for some years: even though we had gained political independence, we were struggling to gain economic independence. And our father's push for African Unity also was a great, great threat to some. The day of the coup was a traumatic one, the kind you don't forget. I remember gunshots in the house where we lived. There was a gun battle and eventually the soldiers of the coup overpowered the presidential guards and ordered us to leave. After the coup, we ended up in prison and were eventually put on a flight to Egypt, our mother's country, where we lived until we were allowed to return to Ghana in 1975.

Our father went to Guinea, to be closer to Ghana, and because Guinea's president was one of his staunchest allies. We never saw him again. The explanation given to us was that it was not safe for us to travel to go and see him, nor was it safe for him to come to us. We talked occasionally and we corresponded, but the family was never reunited, and he passed away six years later in 1972. I remember him calling us on the night of the coup. I was terrified and had been crying that whole day, and he said to me: 'I don't want you to be afraid. I want you to be strong.' That stuck in my mind. Yes, we must be strong.

George Padmore Research Library on
African Affairs, Ghana National Construction
Corporation, Accra, 1961

The design of the Padmore Library is
sometimes attributed to Max Bond, but
is more likely by Nickson and Borys

Temples of a

Chandigarh

New India

(Previous spread) Le Corbusier in Chandigarh with
a plan of the city and a model of the Modulor Man,
his universal system of proportion, 1951

The Capitol Complex viewed from the Secretariat
Building showing, from left to right, the Palace of
Assembly, Tower of Shadows and High Court

The Palace of Assembly viewed
from the Tower of Shadows

Vikramaditya Prakash

Vikramaditya Prakash works on modernism, post-coloniality and global history. Recent books include *One Continuous Line: Art, Architecture and Urbanism of Aditya Prakash* and *Le Corbusier's Chandigarh Revisited: Preservation as Future Modernism*. An ACSA Distinguished Professor, Prakash teaches at the University of Washington, Seattle, is host of the ArchitectureTalk podcast, and co-design lead of O(U)R: Office of (Un)certainty Research.

My father, Aditya Prakash, joined the Chandigarh capital project because he was seduced by the project of nation-building. He was working in the UK in 1952 – in Glasgow, to be precise – but was quite unhappy in that job and was pondering whether to move back to London, or to India, when he heard about Chandigarh. An opportunity to work on the Nehruvian nation-building project felt like a godsend. He knew Maxwell Fry and Jane Drew from his time in London, and when he wrote to them to inquire about it he almost immediately received an invitation to interview, followed a month later by an offer letter.

Those early days in the capital project office were simultaneously heady and testing. The office revolved around Le Corbusier, who held court like the 'master' he considered himself to be. He worked with a self-conscious sense of making history. While Pierre Jeanneret worked hard to mediate between Le Corbusier and the rest of the team, and Fry and Drew variously challenged and deferred to the big man, the nine Indian architects – M.N. Sharma, A.R. Prabhawalkar, B.P. Mathur, Piloo Mody, Eulie Chowdhury, N.S. Lamba, Jeet Malhotra, J.S. Dethe and my father (the most junior in rank) – scrambled to simply tune in to what was going on and to establish their chops.

The engineering office that was responsible for the actual construction was headed by P.L. Varma, a tall, proud man who made it his task to be a foil to Le Corbusier. The administrative head of the project was P.N. Thapar, a bull-headed man accustomed to ordering his juniors around. He held the purse-strings and often ran afoul of the architects. This polyglot, hierarchic team worked literally in a dust field and managed not to disintegrate only because they knew they were supporting the heroic aspirations of the newly independent nation-state. The personal at that time for them was unambiguously political.

Nehru personally took the decision to build Chandigarh as a new Modernist city, both as a retort to Lutyens's and Baker's colonial New

Delhi and as a response to the carnage of Partition. For Nehru and his ilk, it was bad-faith colonialist thinking that had resulted in the partitioning of India with its attendant violence. Reducing people to their religious identity struck Nehru as backward-looking, and prompted his casting of the new Indian nation-state in a firmly secularist mould, with modern architecture adopted as part of its search for new cultural expressions – the making, as he famously put it, of the 'new temples of modern India'.

For Nehru, New Delhi's stripped neo-classicism and beaux-arts axial planning was a naked representation of the Eurocentric ambitions of the colonial project which sought to amalgamate the colonies under the banners and styles of the West. Modern architecture, as a correlate of modern science, technology and reason, represented itself as being universal and in that sense a global heritage as much Indian as western. Post-colonial agency for the Nehruvian nation-state meant having the West on tap, rather than on top. Nehru felt that post-colonial India need suffer no embarrassment in hiring our erstwhile 'masters' (in the political sense) as the new masters (experts). Chandigarh's Modernism was intended by Nehru as a catalyst for change, something to 'make you think' and to be continued by the Indian architects and planners once the hired foreign experts had left. He relied on the Indian 'trainees' to not confuse one sense of mastery with the other – though this, of course, was easier said than done. For my father, the distinction was the foundational responsibility of the post-colonial officer working for the newly independent nation-state; in a sense, his entire career was based on fulfilling this responsibility.

In 1954, barely a year and a half after he had returned to India, my father formed the Modern Architects Club to jump-start the task of taking over the Chandigarh project from the 'foreign experts'. It is important to remember that these foreign experts' contracts stipulated that they were hired for a short period of two to three years to 'train' the Indian architects and planners exactly for this purpose. With Jane Drew's encouragement, my father created this club, as he announced at its inaugural meeting, to respond to the critiques of Chandigarh and to 'set our own house in order'. Nevertheless, it took a very long time for the Indian architects to actually take over the Chandigarh project; Pierre Jeanneret and Le Corbusier continued to dominate it until 1965, when M.N. Sharma became chief architect following Jeanneret's departure.

From his earliest days on the capital project team, my father sought to 'make his mark' by standing out as an original thinker, as for instance in his creation of the Modern Architects Club. He had become obsessed with theatre design during his time in London, and the Tagore Theatre was his breakout project. This was his opportunity to produce his own reading of a perfect acoustic environment, scaled to the size of an intimate performance space. One of his key design conceits was that the spectator was turned around two or three times before they entered the actual theatre, so that they were somewhat disoriented and ready to accept the windowless theatre as a space where miracles might happen. In that sense, the Tagore Theatre was also a reimagining of Le Corbusier's never-realized 'Miracle Box' design.

How to Indianize Modernism was the central topic of conversation in my father's living room throughout the 1970s and early '80s, while he was principal of the Chandigarh College of Architecture. All through that period, a steady stream of visitors from around the world came to see Chandigarh and would inevitably end up in our house. I remember many a night when architects, planners, artists, writers, film-makers and their ilk would be jammed into our living room and, amid interminable rounds of Indian blended Scotch whisky and spicy pakoras made by my weary mother, would contest the best modality of moving beyond Chandigarh and rethinking Modernism for the future.

The Linear City was my father's proposal for Chandigarh 2.0: a tabula rasa city that continued the clear rationalistic design order of

Le Corbusier's masterplan but as a self-sustaining ecosystem. Unlike the Chandigarh that was designed to cater to the upper classes, however, his plan was accommodative of (indeed, reliant on) the vast so-called informal sector that even today supplies the lifeblood that allows the Indian metropolis to function. Formally, his proposal was quite simply to restrict motorized traffic to an elevated tier (on *pilotis* à la Le Corbusier, one might say), liberating the ground plain for non-threatening human- and animal-powered modes of living and transportation, as in pre-industrial India. In a sense he wanted to combine Nehru's aspiration for the future of urban India with that of Mahatma Gandhi, who famously said: 'India lives in its villages.'

It is testimony to the persistence of the neo-colonial framing of our contemporary art world that the creation of Chandigarh remains white-washed and its Indian co-creators relatively unknown. That modern architecture emerged as a response to an industrial culture that was inextricably yoked to the global-colonial, and as such was always already global in character, is an idea that the Eurocentric West has great difficulty with, even today. By contrast, if you look through the archives of architects such as Le Corbusier, Jeanneret, Fry and Drew who were actively working in non-western locations such as India and West Africa, and if you pay careful attention to their characterizations of their modalities of work and (co)creation, you will find that they repeatedly and in different registers give credit to their local collaborators – not always, and not consistently, but happily and willingly.

One would have to say that the 'avant-garde' Modernists of India like my father essentially lost out to the revivalists by the mid-1980s. By then, even storied Indian Modernists such as Charles Correa and Balkrishna Doshi were making buildings based on the 'mandala' and suchlike. That's the milieu in which I went to architecture school, when Chandigarh was castigated not because it was anti-poor and unsustainable, but because it did not 'look' Indian. Having been born and brought up there, I was shocked to hear this. I knew of Chandigarh as nothing other than an Indian city: a proud manifestation of the aspirations of the Nehruvian nation-state.

Neo-liberal India, Modi's India, has unfortunately predicated its identity on the negation of India's Nehruvian/Gandhian past, an entirely unnecessary conceit given that its economic and political priorities emerge out of and build on the institutions that were set up by the Nehruvian nation-state. Their negation of the Nehruvian ethos, as I see it, is classically Oedipal, designed to claim difference by vocal vilification. Unlike many, I do not think that the substantial Nehruvian institutions like democracy, secularism, self-reliance and open discourse are critically at threat in contemporary India. In spite of all the sabre-rattling, I am confident that they will prove to be resilient and emerge strengthened in times to come.

All the sabre-rattling has of course had the unfortunate corollary consequence that many of the more visible symbols of the Nehruvian state, such as its art and architecture, are being besmeared by the current regime, with architecture one of their favourite preoccupations precisely because of its large symbolic power in the public realm, as we learnt from the event of the demolition of Babri Masjid. Chandigarh thus far has not become a target of the neo-nationalists. This may change; but all the buildings in Chandigarh that have been destroyed, including my father's Tagore Theatre, KC Theatre, Jagat Theatre and the petrol pumps, have been at the instigation of local market forces and at the hands of local architects.

The Palace of Assembly, built 1962,
showing brise soleil and other external
shading devices

The High Court, built 1954, showing brise
soleil and the parasol roof suggested by
Fry and Drew

Muslim refugees flee India
by train, 1947

A refugee camp for 300,000 photographed
by Henri Cartier-Bresson, Kurukshetra,
Punjab, 1947

Chapter

After a long freedom struggle, India gained independence on 15 August 1947, ending almost 200 years of British colonial rule. In Parliament House, at the stroke of midnight on the eve of independence, Nehru made his 'Tryst with Destiny' speech: 'A moment comes, but rarely in history, when we step out from the old to the new, when an age ends, and when the soul of a nation, long suppressed, finds utterance,' he proclaimed. He called on India's new citizens to work together to 'bring freedom and opportunity to the common man, to the peasants and workers of India; to fight and end poverty and ignorance and disease; to build up a prosperous, democratic and progressive nation, and to create social, economic and political institutions which will ensure justice and fullness of life to every man and woman'.[1]

When the Indian subcontinent became independent, it was divided into two nations: secular India and Muslim-majority Pakistan. The question was, how to split the disputed provinces of Punjab and Bengal between them? The final boundary, decided by the British and hurriedly drawn up in just five weeks by the barrister Sir Cyril Radcliffe, who had never visited India before (which was partly why he was chosen), was only announced two days after independence was celebrated. Millions of people found themselves forced to move across new national borders, resulting in the largest migration in human history. Around 6.5 million Muslims moved into West Punjab, now part of Pakistan, and 4.7 million Hindus and Sikhs moved into East Punjab, now part of India, amid an atmosphere that has been described as 'retributive genocide'.[2] It is estimated that over a million people died in the ensuing upheaval and sectarian violence.

There is surprisingly little Indian art recording the terrors of Partition. One artist who did seek to capture something of this traumatic time was Satish Gujral, whose father was a freedom fighter and friend of Nehru. Gujral, aged 22 at the time of Partition, worked alongside his father to help refugees flee Pakistan: 'I witnessed killing, murder, rape,' he said. 'I painted the cruelty of man.'[3] Deaf since the age of eight, he watched these crimes as if they were a silent horror movie. His Partition series depicts veiled women in mourning, crumpled to the ground and creased with suffering and anguish. In the 1950s, Gujral – whose brother

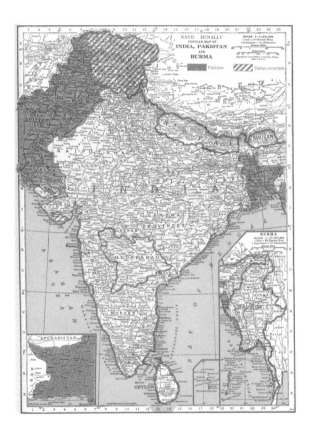

Map of Partition showing the disputed regions of Punjab and Bengal, 1947

Mourning en Masse by
Satish Gujral, 1952

Untitled (Portrait of Nehru)
by Satish Gujral, 1957

would later become Indian prime minister – painted a portrait of Nehru looking down mournfully at a cat's cradle of blood on his hands, as if reflecting on his acceptance of Partition as the price for independence. It was an anti-heroic portrayal that the prime minister, unsurprisingly, rejected.

In Partition the Punjab lost its capital, Lahore – where Gujral had gone to art school – to Pakistan. A new administrative capital was needed for the state, as well as a home for millions of refugees. In response, Nehru planned a new city at Chandigarh, located on a plain at the foothills of the Himalayas. This ambitious resettlement programme became the first Modernist city built from scratch anywhere in the world (predating Brasilia in Brazil), and was independent India's first large-scale project. Nehru also inaugurated the Bhakra Nangal Dam in Punjab, intended to power and irrigate the arid region, celebrating both as 'temples of modern India' that would serve to unify and industrialize the country.[4] At the time, 80 percent of India's population lived in rural areas but – in contrast to Gandhi, who thought that 'the multiplication of wants and machinery' of modernity was 'satanic' and 'baneful' and who celebrated the moral integrity and cottage industries of these villages – Nehru believed that the key to India's post-colonial self-sufficiency was industrial modernity.[5]

Nehru wanted Chandigarh, a city planned for 150,000 people, to overshadow New Delhi, the former imperial capital 400km to its south. The British architect Edwin Lutyens had designed New Delhi in 1912 as an Indian Rome, a physical expression of Britain's power in India; he subsumed Delhi's existing ancient monuments, such as Humayun's Tomb, into his urban plan almost as if they were, as the academic Sunil Khilnani puts it, 'follies on the Imperial estate'.[6] Lutyens, who dismissed Indian architecture as 'cumbrous, ill-constructed … the building style of children', had been pressured by the then Viceroy to work in the revivalist Indo-Saracenic style then favoured by colonialists and Indian elites; reluctantly, the architect merged Classicism with what he considered the 'nobler' features of India's architectural heritage.[7] He quoted the form of a Buddhist stupa, for example, in the dome of Viceroy's House – a political gesture intended to make this expression of imperial might somewhat more palatable to the local population. Despite these

embellishments, Nehru dismissed the result as 'un-Indian'. But the imperial capital was now the inherited seat of Indian power, with the president living in Viceroy's House (renamed Rashtrapati House) and Nehru in his prime ministerial residence at Flagstaff House (Teen Murti Bhavan), the former home of the Commander-in-Chief of the British Indian Army.

Nehru perceived Modernism, although no more Indian than Lutyens's Delhi, as an International Style free from the baggage of the past and from any religious differences, which appealed to his secular, progressive and socialist sensibility. Chandigarh was Nehru's political manifesto, a symbol of change from India's colonial heritage. It was, he declared, 'an expression of the nation's faith in the future … symbolic of the freedom of India, unfettered by the traditions of the past'. The city would be not only 'a soothing balm on the wounded spirit of the Punjab' but a unifying architectural symbol for a new India.[8] Chandigarh, a challenge to the past, was an instrument of Nehru's political propaganda and five-year plans, a showpiece of a new order that promised to restore India's greatness and standing in the world.

Though Chandigarh is inextricably linked with the reputation and legacy of Le Corbusier, the architect's involvement in the project was almost entirely accidental. At first, Nehru refused to believe an Indian architect was not capable of the job; when persuaded otherwise by his bureaucrats, he engaged the American planner Albert Mayer, who had come to India as an army engineer during the war and stayed on, at Nehru's invitation, to build model villages in Uttar Pradesh. Mayer conceived of Chandigarh's urban plan as fan-shaped, divided into super-blocks or sectors. These were detailed by the Polish architect Matthew Nowicki, who had worked with Le Corbusier as a consultant on the design of the UN building in New York, and who imagined the city as a colourful mosaic of neighbourhood units rendered in a deliberately romantic and slightly Disneyfied idiom, with balconies and *jaalis* inspired by traditional Indian architecture. 'I feel we have been able to make it strongly Indian in feeling and function, as well as modern', Mayer wrote to Nehru of this Garden City.[9]

In 1950, however, tragedy struck: Nowicki died in a plane crash en route to New York from Cairo, and a new architect

Miniature showing Lutyens presenting a model of Viceroy's House, New Delhi to the Viceroy, 1931

was needed to help realize the project. Impressed with their Tropical Modernism in West Africa, Nehru sent his emissaries to invite Maxwell Fry and Jane Drew to draw up the architectural designs for Chandigarh in Nowicki's stead. The couple were, as Fry put it, 'coming straight from the easy glories of West Africa where we had reigned supreme'.[10] Nehru had probably heard about them from the German émigré Otto Koenigsberger, then Director of Housing at the Ministry of Health in Delhi where he was doing his own experiments with tropical architecture and planning other Modernist cities: Bhubaneshwar, Bhopal and Gandhinagar. Koenigsberger would move to London in 1952 to advise on Basildon New Town, and in 1957 replaced Fry as Director of the Department of Tropical Architecture at the Architectural Association (AA).

P.L. Varma, the chief engineer of Punjab, and P.N. Thapar, the chief administrator of the Chandigarh Project, were dispatched to London to meet Fry and Drew. Fry was initially reluctant to get involved with Chandigarh, thinking that the practice already had too much work with University College Ibadan in Nigeria and other projects in the Gold Coast, in addition to their work helping to organize and build the 1951 Festival of Britain on London's South Bank. 'When the couple asked for time to make their decision, the Indian delegation apparently sat on the floor – 'in almost yogic poses', according to Drew – and said that they would wait until Drew and Fry had made up their minds.[11] Drew persuaded her husband to accept, and the couple invited Denys Lasdun and Lindsay Drake to join their architectural partnership to take care of other work as they prepared for India and new adventures. 'Impulsive by nature and romantic at heart, Jane Drew was enthusiastic about the new capital and wanted to go to India,' Fry wrote.[12]

At Drew and Fry's suggestion, they and the Indian team travelled to France to recruit their hero, the influential Swiss-born French architect Le Corbusier, then aged 63. When Thapar questioned the benefit of asking Le Corbusier to join the project, Fry replied that it would bring 'Honour and glory for you, and an unpredictable portion of misery for me'.[13] As they expected, Le Corbusier, the grand old man of the Congrès Internationaux

Caricature bust of Lutyens
with pith helmet based
on the dome of Viceroy's
House, 1917

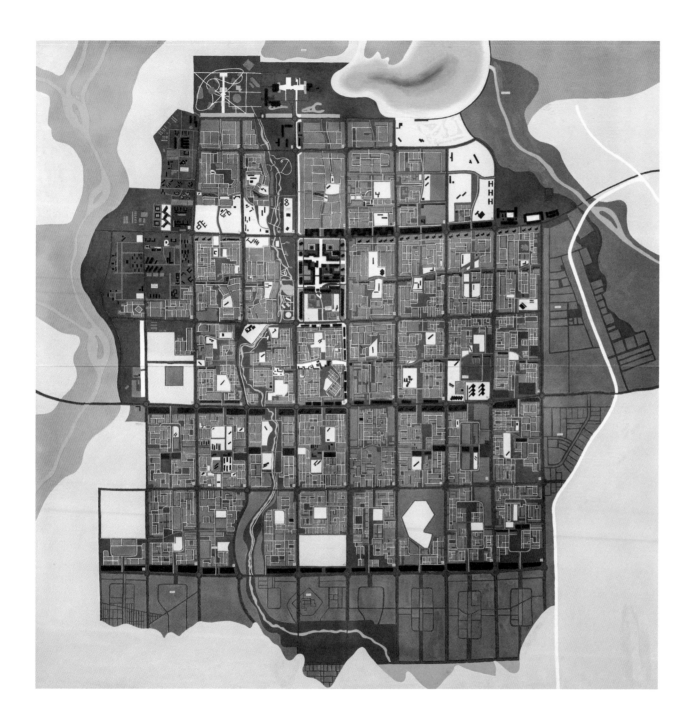

Reproduction of a 1950s relief model
showing Le Corbusier's gridded plan
for Chandigarh, 2023

Le Corbusier, Drew and Fry relax
on a rug, 1946

The Architects' Office at
Chandigarh including Jane Drew and
Maxwell Fry, A.R. Prabhawalkar and
B.P. Mathur, 1950s

d'Architecture Moderne (CIAM) leapt at the chance to build his ideal 'Radiant City' in India, an opportunity that had evaded him elsewhere, but he was never going to share the acclaim. 'It is the hour that I have been waiting for,' he said, 'India, that humane, profound civilization [which] hadn't yet created an architecture for modern civilization' presented him with what he considered a tabula rasa.[14] Le Corbusier thought Chandigarh would be his 'crowning achievement': it is 'a great victory for CIAM and an opportunity to show that the participants of CIAM are capable of real action', he wrote.[15] Drew later said of Le Corbusier's egomaniacal nature: 'It was clear after a while that he was really a dictator at heart … He was so sure architects could change the pattern of life and should be given the power to do it.'[16]

Le Corbusier signed a contract as Architectural Advisor to Punjab, with the stipulation that he only had to visit India twice a year. He nominated his cousin Pierre Jeanneret as his representative in India. Le Corbusier and Jeanneret had worked together for 20 years before disagreements caused a parting of ways in 1940, so for Jeanneret this was both reunion and exile. Le Corbusier agreed to join the Chandigarh project if he could design the more glamorous public buildings in the Capitol Complex, or administrative centre, posting his designs from his studio in Paris. He would leave the rest of the city to Fry, Drew and Jeanneret, all three of whom were hired as Senior Architects, effectively working under Varma. Jeanneret and Fry were in their early fifties; Drew had just turned 40. Jeanneret wrote to Le Corbusier that it was 'two against one, including one woman – and I believe a rather scheming one at that'.[17] Fry and Drew lived in Chandigarh from 1951 until they left in 1955, while Jeanneret made the city his permanent home until his death in 1965, when his ashes were scattered there in Sukhna Lake.

On arrival in Chandigarh in 1951, and having had little engagement with the place, Le Corbusier immediately set about sketching an alternative vision planned on a strict Modernist grid and soon ousted Albert Mayer from the project. 'Corbusier held the crayon in his hand and was in his element,' recalled Fry. '"*Voilà la gare*," he said, "*et voici la rue commerciale*," and he drew the first road on the new plan of Chandigarh. "*Voici la tête*," he went on, indicating

Enamel door for the Palace of
Assembly with solar imagery painted
by Le Corbusier, 1962

A panel depicts the four European
architects as animals

84

with a smudge the higher ground to the left of Mayer's location, the ill effects of which I had already pointed out to him. *"Et voilà l'estomac, le cité-centre."*[18]

Le Corbusier designed the city as a living organism: the Capitol Complex would be the head and brains of Chandigarh; the heart was the city's commercial district, fed by the roads which were this urban body's veins and which delineated its 30 sectors; the city's green avenues and parks were its lungs. Le Corbusier set about designing the most important site, the brains of the city, conceived as a kind of concrete Acropolis set against the dramatic backdrop of the Himalayan foothills that would proclaim the power of the people in this new democracy.

Drew, Fry and Jeanneret designed the bulk of Chandigarh – the less showy schools, colleges, hospitals, cinemas and over 14 types of sustainable houses for different socio-economic groups, which were constructed on stringent budgets. The austere 'Chandigarh Style' they established used local materials to respond to the climate (which was cold in winter but extremely hot in summer), with brick brise soleil screens, deep-set windows, and roof terraces for sleeping on in humid weather, and exerted a huge influence on social housing in the Nehru years.

Sector 22 was the first to be completed and Le Corbusier said that it was the first cheap housing he'd seen that didn't look cheap. The buildings looked inwards, and like all the other sectors was fairly self-contained, with heavy traffic restricted to the perimeter. The green had a view of the Himalayas and swimming baths, nurseries and a health centre were all within a quarter of a mile (400m) of each dwelling. The Indian architect Charles Correa would later criticize the way that each sector was a miniature world cut off from the others and lacking 'the interaction – and the synergy – that we love about cities'.[19]

Houses in Chandigarh were arranged in sectors moving downward from the Capitol according to one's status and income, from rich to poor, from houses for government officials to those for peons and tanga drivers. Jeanneret's own house was in Sector 5 alongside those of other top government officials, but though these occupied considerably larger sites, even these had few luxuries; now a museum and guesthouse, it has curving fieldstone walls like inverted parentheses, polished concrete floors and generous balconies with latticed screens made of bricks stacked on their sides, lending it a simple grandeur.

Le Corbusier, who stayed in Jeanneret's home when in Chandigarh, would satirize the four European architects in the enamel door covered in solar symbols that he painted in 1962. It provides a splash of vivid colour under the parasol roof of the Palace of Assembly, as the seat of Chandigarh's government is known. In one of the 55 exterior panels, which also contains his signature, Le Corbusier paints himself as a crow, the translation of his pseudonym ('Corbu'); Pierre Jeanneret is portrayed as a French cockerel, pecking around in the dirt, Jane Drew as a goat and, somewhat rudely, Maxwell Fry as a kid suckling her udders. Drew might have suggested altogether different animal comparisons: she called Jeanneret 'a diminutive, little man rather like a monkey and a little like Corb to look at'.[20] In her unpublished diaries there are hints of an affair with Le Corbusier, which made Fry unbelievably jealous. 'Despite his elevated thoughts and passionate nature, [Le Corbusier] was finally nothing more than a very close friend,' Drew wrote in a chapter of her unpublished memoir called 'Loves'.[21]

Drew and Fry explained to Le Corbusier the principles of climate control they had developed in their work in West Africa, and the influence of their ideas on his Indian work has perhaps been underestimated. Based on British expertise in tropical architecture, as well as his own experience in North Africa and Brazil, Le Corbusier sought to make prototypes for 'modern architecture in the Indian climate'.[22] The French, of course, had experience of building in the Tropics, in Africa's French colonies: Le Corbusier's friend Jean Prouvé, a frequent visitor to Chandigarh, designed prefabricated buildings, such as his Maison Tropicale and Sahara House, for use in Congo and Algeria. For Africa, Prouvé proposed the mass production of aluminium roofs, which would crown traditional earth structures and be the first step in creating new housing schemes for the continent in accordance with CIAM principles. However, even he genuflected to Fry and Drew's work in his own experiments with passive cooling, and the book he published in 1958, *Habitat et urbanism en zone tropicale humide:*

Models of Le Corbusier's
Legislative Assembly (left) and
Tower of Shadows (above) by Giani
Rattan Singh, 1957

Cover of *Marg* magazine, 1961, devoted to
Chandigarh, featuring Le Corbusier's tapestry
designed for the High Court Building (right,
photographed by Jeet Malhotra), shown with the
architects' camp in the foreground, 1955

SITTING 1ST ROW

Jagjit Singh, Khem Chand, M.L. Sharma, R.L. Mathur, S.P. Bhasin, J.N. Seth, R.P. Sachdev, S.N. Amin, V.P. Sanon, R. Bahadur, R.P. Chinda, K.K. Saini, Sher Jang

CHAIRS 2ND ROW

S.K. Dutta (Asst. Architect), Surjit Singh (Asst. Architect), M.S. Siali (Asst. Architect), R.R. Handa (Jr. Architect), B.P. Mathur (Jr. Architect), J.S. Dethe (Jr. Town Planner), P. Jeanneret (Senr. Architect), E. Maxwell Fry (Senr. Architect), Jane B. Drew

(Senr. Architect), N.S. Lamba (Jr. Town Planner), A.R. Prabhawalker (Jr. Town Planner), H.S. Dinsa (Landscape Architect), J.L. Malhotra (Asst. Architect), S.G. Nangia (Asst. Town Planner), V.P. Dhamija (Asst. Architect)

3RD ROW STANDING

S.D. Sharma, Milik Singh Kuhli, Iqbal Singh, Ram Kishan, Chandu Lal, Hans Raj, Jai Gopal, V.S. Puri, Udaybir Singh, S.N. Madan, Harbans Lal, B.R. Sharma, Prem Parkash, M.L. Madan, Balbir Singh, Pran Nath, Nathu Ram, Karam Singh, Pyara Singh, N.V. Shastri

4TH ROW STANDING

M.N. Nair, Jashir Singh Sachdev, M.S. Jhashi, G.D. Mathur, Jagdish Singh, Balwant Singh, V.V. Bodas, M.D. Mande, Jagdish Chander, Khushal Chand, Parshotam Singh Kodle, M.P. Gupta, Hem Chand, Rattan Singh, Gurbachan Singh, Mast Ram, Kishan Chand

5TH ROW STANDING

Bhagat Ram, Harsaroop, Suram Singh, Birdu RaPaPm, Jewan Singh, Ram Dass I, Ram Dass II, Chand Ram, Sardha Singh, Hari Dass, Thakar Dass, D. Jagat Singh, Sahib Singh, Dhani Singh, Sukh Dev

elements d'une doctrine d'action (Housing and Urbanism in the Humid Tropical Zone: Elements of an Action Plan), leaned liberally on the ideas expounded by Fry and Drew in *Tropical Architecture in the Humid Zone* (1956), even to the extent of reproducing some of its illustrations.

In dialogue with Fry and Drew, Le Corbusier designed a large experimental structure that he called the Tower of Shadows. He had a model of it made to explore the principles of climate control essential to Tropical Modernism, arranging deep louvres that mimicked the thick mud walls of traditional houses to illustrate how, as he put it, 'the sun can be controlled at all four cardinal points of an edifice and even manipulated in a hot country to reduce temperatures'.[23] The architect saw this porous, airy pavilion as a practical experiment in climate science that informed his other Chandigarh designs: for example, the Secretariat, a horizontal skyscraper 245m long and 45m high, uses similar brise soleils to screen the sun and articulate the building. The High Court also has a huge parasol canopy to allow for the cooling effect of moving air under shaded conditions, an idea suggested by Fry and Drew. The Tower of Shadows, a study in light, shade and wind, was eventually built as a sort of solar monument in front of the Palace of Assembly, along the lines of the Jantar Mantar observatory Le Corbusier had admired and sketched in Delhi. 'The climate has been the determining factor in Chandigarh architecture,' wrote Fry approvingly, 'and so it should be.'[24]

Nehru later confessed that he didn't like all the buildings in Chandigarh, though he liked some very much, declaring the Secretariat 'magnificent' and the High Court 'grand' (Fry considered the former 'too long' and the latter 'too theatrical', criticisms which stung Le Corbusier and were perhaps meant to).[25] Nehru, who 'discovered' India after his schooling in the West, thought that the country had stagnated even before colonialism, a slumber that the colonialists perpetuated and exploited, and was 'eager and anxious to change her outlook and appearance and give her the garb of modernity'.[26] Similarly, Le Corbusier had a romantic, mystical idea of India as a timeless country that was 'awakening, intact' in the 'Second Machine Age', having sleepwalked through the first.[27] He hoped that an alternative modernity might grow there which would avoid the mistakes of a capitalist West with which he was increasingly disillusioned.

This echoed his earlier experience of designing in Algeria in the 1930s, where he generated Plan Obus, a viaduct city skirting the Casbah in the Cape of Algiers – a project for the French colonial government that was abandoned during the war. 'Arabs, are there no peoples but you who dwell in coolness and quiet, in the enchantment of proportions and the savour of a humane architecture?' he asked, contrasting the vernacular architecture of North Africa with Paris, 'where "civilized" people are holed up like rats'.[28] Admiring of the mud forms of local Punjabi architecture, he brought to India a similarly orientalizing vision. Le Corbusier praised Chandigarh's 'eternal landscape': 'Everything is calm, slow, harmonious, loveable'.[29]

★

By 1947 India had a population of about 330 million, but only 300 qualified architects. Almost half of them worked in Bombay, where Art Deco predominated. Nehru insisted that the European architects at Chandigarh employ Indian staff rather than bring their own offices to India; he wanted it to be a 'living school' for local architects, who would train on the job, thereby upskilling a new generation. 'We are to create an architectural centre in India mainly with young Hindus with foreign diplomas who will form the Planning Office for the Punjab Capital,' wrote Le Corbusier of this team of young architects, most of whom had trained abroad, describing his role to them as that of 'friendly shepherd'.[30] Fry and Drew's contracts also specified that they would train an Indian workforce. In the Architects' Office (see opposite, 1954), the first building to be constructed at Chandigarh, Fry and Drew had large interconnected offices with a shared hatch, in which was a telephone. Drew at first claimed that their Indian architectural support was 'woefully inadequate', but later acknowledged the 'tremendous and devoted support of our, for the most part, inexperienced and only partially trained Indian staff'.[31]

A 1961 issue of *Marg*, the magazine of the Modern Architectural Research Group (MARG) founded in Bombay by Mulk Raj Anand in 1946, celebrated the achievements of these Indian 'founders of Chandigarh'.[32] *Marg*, of which Minnette de Silva was architectural

Golconde Guesthouse by
Antonin Raymond (drawing by François
Sammer), Pondicherry, 1937–42

The Architects' Office
at Chandigarh, 1950s

Ahmedabad Textile Industry's
Research Association (ATIRA) designed
by Achyut Kanvinde, Ahmedabad, 1950–4

editor, opposed the 'slavish mentality' of colonialism, from which it was hoped Modernism would allow a release.[33] Rather than seeing Chandigarh as a gift or imposition by European Modernists, part of the International Style's global spread, *Marg* made clear that these Indian 'torch-bearers of modernism' co-created the city by treating them on a par with the European architects. Chandigarh was a product of the post-colonial condition, which presented the unique conditions for its creation and Le Corbusier with an unprecedented opportunity. As architect Charles Correa put it: 'India was lucky to get Le Corbusier; Le Corbusier was lucky to get India.'[34]

So blinded are most historians by the supernova that is Le Corbusier that, even inside India, these architects have been little recognized for their contribution to Chandigarh and India's cultural identity post-independence. They include M.N. Sharma, A.R. Prabhawalkar, Eulie Chowdhury, Shivdatt Sharma, B.P. Mathur, Piloo Mody, Aditya Prakash, J.S. Dethe, N.S. Lamba, J.K. Chowdhury, Jeet Malhotra, Mahendra Raj and, working from Paris in Le Corbusier's studio, Balkrishna Doshi. This generation of talented young practitioners, who cut their teeth constructing the new city, went on to build much of modern India. Many of them would become critical of Le Corbusier's legacy and seek to escape his influence, fusing the lessons of his sculptural function-alism with a greater sensitivity to India's architectural heritage and social context to create a unique tropical style.

Interviewed by the author in 2023, the then 92-year-old architect Shivdatt Sharma, who began his career building Chandigarh, and was one of the nine first Indian architects employed there, recalled: 'All Indian architects at that time had been trained in Europe because there were no registered colleges of architecture in India. That is why they could follow Modernism very conveniently.'[35] Modernist ideas were not foreign to the Indian architects: 'Modernism is a European thought,' he notes, 'propagated religiously by Le Corbusier – but Le Corbusier only reinforced the idea of Modernism, it was already here.' For example, buildings such as Antonin Raymond's Golconde Guesthouse in Pondicherry, completed in 1942, with its walls of asbestos louvres, already contained the core principles that would become known

Eulie Chowdhury and Jeanneret
with model of the Assembly
Building, 1950s

Library chair designed by
Chowdhury and Jeanneret, c.1955

as Tropical Modernism (it is unclear if Fry and Drew knew of this important precedent). Otto Koenigsberger, who had worked for architect Ernst May in Frankfurt and with Minnette de Silva in India, had also built Modernist buildings in Mysore and elsewhere which responded to climate; and Gira Sarabhai and Achyut Kanvinde, who had both trained in America, built Modernist buildings in Ahmedabad long before Le Corbusier had the chance to design there.

Sharma, who had studied architecture at Delhi Polytechnic, was employed in Chandigarh as an Assistant Architect. He was one of the few architects to have learned his practice exclusively in India, on the job there. 'I liked Modernism because it is functional – buildings must fulfil their function,' Sharma says. Eventually he was allowed to work under Le Corbusier on the Government Museum, for which Satish Gujral, after an apprenticeship in Mexico to Diego Rivera, created striking murals in his new role as artist in the Punjab government, Nehru having decreed that one percent of construction costs should go on public art to decorate the buildings.

Like all the Indian architects, Sharma was drilled in the proportional harmony of Le Corbusier's Modulor: the figure of a six-foot man (allegedly the height of detectives in the English crime novels Le Corbusier enjoyed) with large calves, a thin waist and a raised, lobster claw-like hand, around which Le Corbusier designed his buildings. Le Corbusier's drawing of this imaginary figure, which he claimed he used to put humans at the centre of his designs, is still pinned to Sharma's noticeboard today. 'Modernism is an idea, realized by applying Modulor dimensions,' Sharma explains; using these principles, he was able to realize the Chandigarh Architecture Museum after Le Corbusier's death, fulfilling the Frenchman's plans from the loosest of his sketches.

Most of the other Chandigarh architects had trained abroad, the majority in Britain, but had not completed their accreditation. Drew recalled: 'None of the Indian staff except Eulie Chowdhury, who was a sophisticated person and whose father had been an ambassador, were fully qualified architects.'[36] Chowdhury, the daughter of an Indian diplomat posted to Japan and Australia, where she studied architecture, had also lived in the USA and was the only Indian woman on the Chandigarh team (Jane Drew was the only other female architect working on the project, though all correspondence was addressed to her as 'Respected Sir'). Chowdhury, who was herself known for her 'imposing personality' and 'bohemian and unconventional lifestyle', remarked of Drew: 'Her capacity to outrage made her a legend in Chandigarh … she wore very short skirts, which caused a sensation amidst the sari-clad women covered from top to toe.'[37]

Chowdhury's fluent French made her an important link between the French and Indian architects and she helped Le Corbusier with his correspondence to Nehru, who intervened on the architect's behalf at strategic moments in the project: to sack an administrator and restore another to their post, for example, or to kill plans for an army camp that would have marred the view of the Himalayas from Sukhna Lake. When Le Corbusier encountered such issues, he made a note in his diary: 'Write to Nehru.'[38] Chowdhury contributed to the design of Le Corbusier's Capitol Complex, working on the unrealized Governor's Palace with its horn-like canopy. However, this project was vetoed by Nehru as an undemocratic gesture amid a housing crisis, the palace being considered too large a residence for a regional administrator, especially in Punjab with its large volume of refugees.

To replace the Governor's Palace, Le Corbusier began designs for a Museum of Knowledge, a technological centre that would help members of the Assembly next door to make scientifically informed decisions. Chowdhury also worked on these designs. It was to be, Le Corbusier wrote to Nehru in 1960, 'an Electronic Laboratory of scientific decision put at the disposal of authority and destined to assure the execution of useful orders concerning the part of the life of the country which is called its urbanism'.[39] However, this techno-utopian idea was also never realized and the land lies empty, leaving Le Corbusier's vision for the Capitol incomplete. In her own right Chowdhury designed many other Chandigarh buildings, including the Government Polytechnic College for Women, whose dormitories had zigzagging balconies where students could sleep outside in the hot months. She also designed some of the famous Chandigarh chairs, until recently solely attributed to Pierre Jeanneret. Chowdhury went on to

become the chief state architect of Punjab and Haryana, where she oversaw the second phase of Chandigarh's development.

When independence was declared, Aditya Prakash, who had also studied architecture at Delhi Polytechnic, was on the boat to London, where he attended evening classes at the Regent Street Polytechnic as well as lectures about Modernism at the AA. After an interview with Maxwell Fry, then on leave in London, he returned to India in 1952 to join the Chandigarh team. He worked with Jane Drew on the General Hospital and various housing projects, and with Le Corbusier on the Government College of Art, before being given his own independent projects. 'Le Corbusier wanted to show a modern democratic India, and he succeeds by using equal elements to create a rippling, beautiful rhythm,' Prakash recalled, adding, less effusively: 'He was rather brash and impatient – he treated us like uninitiated children – but he helped us to realise our own country.'[40]

In 1954, encouraged by Drew, Prakash set up the Modern Architects Club in Chandigarh to provide a forum for the Indian architects working on the project. Among its recommendations was that a School of Architecture should be established in the city, to build on the Chandigarh experiment. 'We Indian Architects who have been associated with the foreign geniuses found ourselves pulsating with life, for such opportunity is very rare in the lives of most Architects,' Prakash wrote, emphasizing the Indian contribution to Chandigarh. 'We have been absorbing the ideas given to us by our visiting Architects, but not only that, we have always had our own contribution, not a small one, to make the most of the buildings built or being built in Chandigarh. Thus, we are proud to say that we proved ourselves worthy of standing up to the world's most renowned Architects.'[41]

Prakash adapted Le Corbusier's Modulor figure to Indian brick sizes, reducing its scale in what his son, the architectural historian Vikramaditya Prakash, has interpreted as a subversive gesture. Using this system, in 1961 he built the Chandigarh College of Architecture, the crowning achievement of the Modern Architecture Club, as a proportionally smaller copy of Le Corbusier's art college in an adjacent sector. Searching for his own expression, Aditya Prakash departed from Le Corbusier's influence with the Tagore Theatre, also completed in 1961 for the centenary of the poet and playwright Rabindranath Tagore, who had invited the Bauhaus to exhibit in Calcutta in 1922. Jeanneret, preferring Prakash's design over his own, had awarded the younger man the commission – a generous gesture for which Prakash felt indebted. There is a photograph of someone lifting up the roof of a model of the structure, which juxtaposes two squares on their diagonal axis; the modelmaker is hidden from sight, with only their hands visible, which lends the image a surreal air. In 2008 the theatre was gutted, and today only the exterior remains. Prakash was also responsible for other cultural centres, including the Neelam, Jagat and KC theatres, the latter now also demolished.

The landscaping of 'The City Beautiful', as Chandigarh came to be known, was done by the botanist M.S. Randhawa, who had been Deputy Commissioner of Delhi and was then appointed Director-General of Rehabilitation, in charge of resettling Punjabis uprooted by Partition. Randhawa, who became Chandigarh's first chief commissioner, designed the Leisure Valley and Rose Garden as the lungs of the city and gave each street a distinct character with a different colour of flowering tree. These acted as a verdant buffer to ensure that housing sectors were an oasis of calm protected from traffic. In the 1960s Randhawa became a force behind India's Green Revolution, overseeing Nehru's plans for the industrialization of agriculture in the Punjab. Meanwhile, Aditya Prakash left Chandigarh in 1963 to design the region's main campus, Punjab Agricultural University in Ludhiana – an experience that gave him a transformative outside perspective on Chandigarh.

Speaking at Chandigarh in 1995, the academic and theorist Gayatri Chakravorty Spivak criticized the 'obstinate lingering of *guruvada* [guru worship] worn like a badge of honour by Le Corbusier's associates'.[42] Even Prakash – who became critical of Le Corbusier's suburban vision for Chandigarh, developing an almost Oedipal reaction against the 'Master' – referred to Le Corbusier as a guru and thought of the Chandigarh experiment as a kind of architectural ashram, spreading the word of Modernism in India. All the Indian architects competed for the

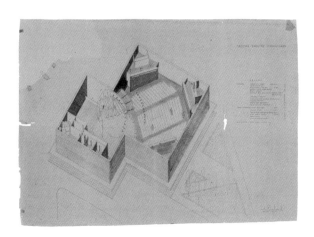

Axonometric section of the Tagore Theatre by Aditya Prakash, *c.*1960

Model of the Tagore Theatre by Giani Rattan Singh, photographed by Aditya Prakash, *c.*1960

Photographs by Jeet Malhotra of
Chandigarh under construction,
including the Assembly Tower (above)
Secretariat (top), peon housing
(middle) and a secondary school
(right), 1951–66

opportunity to work with Le Corbusier on his biannual visits from Paris (even though, as Sharma recalled, he 'had neither the patience nor the temperament to teach'), and for favour with the other European architects. Nehru's 'planned hybridity' failed, Spivak said, because it failed to 'put decolonisation on stage'; he had wanted Chandigarh to represent a new dawn for India, showing a post-colonial way forward, but it merely represented 'the west on tap rather than on top'.[43]

In 1955 Le Corbusier's official photographer Lucien Hervé visited Chandigarh to attend the inauguration of the High Court and to document the new city. Hervé's images, with their characteristically abstract and constructivist stylization, were reproduced widely in the international media and were the world's first encounter with the project. But Hervé only spent a short amount of time in India and a junior architect called Jeet Malhotra took over photographing the construction processes, including his own buildings. These included, with Jeanneret, the Postgraduate Medical Education and Research Institute and, in Malhotra's own right, the Institute's research blocks and auditorium. While Hervé's photographs focused on the geometric beauty of Le Corbusier's buildings, Malhotra's capture the messy everyday life of the creation of a city.

Early images of Chandigarh show an arid plain with little ground cover, covered in the tents of both refugees, architects and construction workers. Concrete edifices rise around them in what looks like an inhospitable space. Jane Drew marvelled at the almost medieval methods of the Chandigarh workforce: 'We found in India that it was cheaper to use seven hundred people to excavate than to employ an excavating machine! Le Corbusier's High Court and Secretariat were built with the aid of donkeys, men, women and children.'[44] A shop in Mall Road in Shimla, which served as the temporary capital of the Punjab while a new one was built, was taken over to advertise Chandigarh and encourage residents to move there. A large-scale plan of the city was on display along with images of completed buildings, and there was also a large picture of a gushing water pipe to reassure people that there was no scarcity of water. Varma diverted a river to create the artificial Sukhna Lake (surrounded by a wide promenade which Le Corbusier helped design), amplifying this image of aquatic abundance.

In 2020 Malhotra recalled the examination that he and other students were set as they competed to join the Chandigarh project. He had to design a low-budget house, a task with which he was familiar having already had a job with Koenigsberger at the Ministry of Health working on resettlement projects for refugees. When the European architects came to inspect the results, Malhotra remembers asking Fry why, if India had built the Taj Mahal, no Indian architect could be found to lead the Chandigarh project. Drew insisted that her husband reply to his expression of 'national pride', and Malhotra received a speedy lecture about the Bauhaus and the Tropical Modernist principles of climate control.[45] Drew later remarked that instead of Le Corbusier, Nehru might have employed Achyut Kanvinde, who had trained with Walter Gropius in America before returning to India after independence to build elegant Modernist buildings in Ahmedabad. Kanvinde was 'a good architect', she wrote, attributing Nehru's oversight to an inferiority complex: 'They had no faith in their own people, you had to be foreign to be good.'[46]

★

Although he would eventually return to Chandigarh to start his own practice, Shivdatt Sharma had to leave for a while to escape Le Corbusier's influence – 'to discover my identity', as he put it.[47] By the late 1960s the 'Chandigarh Style' was being emulated elsewhere in India, in new capitals such as Gandhinagar, Faridabad and Gandhidham, and their practical training and experience ensured that Chandigarh's Indian architects were much in demand. Sharma became chief architect for the Indian Space Research Organisation (ISRO), headquartered in Bangalore, which had been set up by the Ahmedabad patron and physicist Vikram Sarabhai. There, Sharma established his own Chandigarh-like office, and over the next nine years designed major campuses around India for ISRO. He explained that he wanted to create 'inner spaces' of calm and relaxation for employees who lived so much of their working lives focused on 'outer space'. It was, as Balkrishna Doshi put it, 'very different work' from that at Chandigarh, and allowed Sharma to develop his own idiom.[48]

Remembering his time at Chandigarh, and Le Corbusier's giant presence there, Sharma recalled that the Sikh model maker Giani Rattan Singh 'could read Le Corbusier's drawings better than any architect and from them produce meticulous, precise, perfect models'.[49] Constructing Chandigarh, Le Corbusier used these models (now scattered in museums around the world) to study aesthetics, to test designs, proportions and the path of the sun around the buildings, and as a reference point for the other architects and engineers. Working from the drawings Le Corbusier sent from Paris, Singh carefully crafted a plan of his model city in miniature: intricate versions of the Tower of Shadows as well as Chandigarh's High Court, Palace of Assembly, Secretariat and unbuilt Governor's House, fabricated in plaster, teak, Himalayan cedar and kail wood.

Little recognized for his contribution to Chandigarh, Giani Rattan Singh was born in 1908 in Daulatpur in the Punjab into a family of carpenters. In his twenties he moved to Shimla and found work at Viceregal Lodge, the summer residence of the British monarch's representative in India. It was here, in 1945, that the plan for India's self-determination was conceived, and the disputed border between India and Pakistan later decided. A doll's house Singh had made, based on Viceregal Lodge, had pride of place in the hallway of the nineteenth-century colonial building, which was designed in the Jacobethan style. Matthew Nowicki had seen Singh's creation and invited him to join their Chandigarh team. After Nowicki's death, Le Corbusier, similarly impressed with Singh's work, appointed him Head Draughtsman, tasked with constructing models of his large-scale structures.

Singh lived behind the Architects' Office with the rest of the Indian team in leaky tents that had been turned down by refugees, even through the cold Punjabi winters (they were in time rehoused in Sector 22, the first to be built in Chandigarh, so were guinea pigs for the new designs). The Architects' Office, now the Le Corbusier Centre, was itself a practical experiment in the use of eggcrate brise soleils, jute-lined ceilings, clerestory windows and lightweight, concrete-shell canopies. It was built on an alluvial plain surrounded by the bulldozed remnants of some 24 Punjabi villages whose 9,000 residents were compensated a pittance for

Giani Rattan Singh, Head Draughtsman at Chandigarh, known for his intricate architectural models in wood, 1960

Giani Rattan Singh working on
models of the Capitol Complex
assisted by Dhani Ram, 1960

Giani Rattan Singh at the
Architects' Office, with two
components of a model for
the Capitol Complex

the demolition of their mud and thatch homes and their forced resettlement elsewhere. One of the nearby surviving villages was Chandi Mandir, named after the goddess from which Chandigarh also took its name. Here, the Europeans lived in a rest house in relative comfort, with an entitlement of seven servants, along with the chief administrator, P.N. Thapar, and the chief engineer, P.L. Varma (they were eventually rehoused in Sector 19).

'I don't think I have ever met such enthusiasm or hard work as that shown by us and the entire staff during those first three years,' wrote Drew:

> The ground around was littered with the poor workmen and their families, who had no tents to sleep in though they made themselves some sort of cover with the straw; about three feet high wigwams into which they crawled when it was very cold. Men, women, children and babies were on the building site, scaffolding of bamboo poles was tied together in the manner seen in early Italian paintings but the women some from Rajasthan looked like queens with beautifully coloured shirts, anklets and bracelets and carry buckets of concrete on their heads. Babies hung on the scaffolding and were given a slight push now and then by the workmen.[50]

In 1966, a year after Le Corbusier's death, the construction of Chandigarh was not yet complete but it already had 120,000 inhabitants, and by the end of the decade over 200,000. That year, Swiss filmmaker Alain Tanner visited the site and filmed the construction workers passing baskets of concrete up towers of bamboo scaffolding. In his narration, the art critic John Berger described how 'the city was built by hand and carried on the heads of women'. Le Corbusier also described 'teams of women dressed in the wildest colours, carrying in baskets on their heads, the earth of the foundations and relaying each other in a chain that was like a hallucination … the loveliest fabrics dyed brilliant colours'.[51] The film shows the new Chandigarh College of Architecture, with its many students standing at draughtmen's desks in neat rows as they work with concentration on their drawings with T-squares and triangles.

Singh's son, the architect Jaswinder Singh, later lived in the house his father eventually bought for his family in Chandigarh. Its design had been signed off by Pierre Jeanneret, then chief architect: 'It is good for Rattan Singh.'[52] Jeanneret worked closely with Singh, for whom he had great respect, and was a frequent visitor to his workshop on the top floor of the building, occasionally bringing Le Corbusier. Alongside designs for Le Corbusier, Singh made numerous architectural models for Jeanneret, as well as prototypes of the famous teak and rattan 'Chandigarh Chairs' that he made with Eulie Chowdhury. With his assistant Dhani Ram, he also made a pedal boat that Jeanneret designed for use on Sukhna Lake (a reproduction of the boat is in the Jeanneret Museum). There is a photograph of Jeanneret and Le Corbusier launching it successfully under the makers' watchful eyes.

Jaswinder Singh owns an album, hand-made by his father and bound with wire between plywood boards, which records Giani Rattan Singh's work and collaboration with Le Corbusier and the Indian 'founders of Chandigarh'. Singh is shown towering like a giant over a model of the Governor's House, the palace Nehru vetoed as undemocratic. He is photographed alongside Le Corbusier inspecting a model of the High Court, displayed high on a trestle table so that they can peer in through its fin-like columns. In another image, Singh lifts a large model of the funnel which sits on top of the Palace of Assembly, apparently inspired by the cooling towers of the new thermal power station he had seen in Ahmedabad, so that Le Corbusier can inspect the interior. There are also photographs of models of Fry's Government Printing Press, Shivdatt Sharma's hospital cafeteria and guesthouse with its spiralling ramp, and Eulie Chowdhury's campus for the Government Polytechnic College for Women.

In 1952 Singh's models, along with a large number of architecture drawings, were displayed in the chief engineer's office to sell Nehru on the ambitious, radical plans for Chandigarh. 'The design was explained in broad terms, without delving much into the aspect of aesthetics,' recalls M.N. Sharma, who had graduated from the University of Leicester and, after failing to get a job in Fry and Drew's London office, was encouraged to return to Punjab to work on Chandigarh following a chance meeting with the Indian High Commissioner.[53] In June 1950 he became the first Indian architect to be appointed to the Chandigarh team, working with Nowicki and then directly under Le Corbusier and Jeanneret. 'After about 45 minutes of viewing the exhibition,' Sharma recalled, 'Pandit Nehru showed his appreciation and gave his approval on the spot.'[54] In October 1953 Nehru returned to inaugurate the new capital, bringing with him his mistress, Lady Mountbatten. He laid the foundation stone of the Secretariat Building and reassured refugee families that Chandigarh would be even better than Lahore.

Jaswinder Singh kept several gifts Le Corbusier sent his father, including a 1955 book on his architecture and a 1955 cutting from Italian newspaper *La Tribuna*, both of which featured pictures of 'Le Corbusier's Sikh modelmaker' with his gleaming white turban and handsome beard. The inscriptions to Singh are signed 'friendly' by the architect. 'He didn't do that with any other member of the Indian team, even the chief architect or senior architects,' Jaswinder Singh says proudly of the two men's special relationship. 'Le Corbusier didn't know Punjabi and my father didn't know French, but they both spoke the language of architectural models and drawings fluently.'[55]

M.N. Sharma, who would become the city's chief architect after Jeanneret and a fierce defender of Le Corbusier's urban values, wrote: 'Giani Rattan Singh deserves special mention as the most versatile in assisting Le Corbusier by making accurate models of the buildings. He also helped me and other architects. In recognition of his meritorious service, I employed him even after his retirement until he was unable to work given his deteriorating eyesight. I also recommended his son to serve in his place.'[56] Following in his father's footsteps, and having learned by assisting him, Jaswinder Singh worked as a modelmaker in the chief architect's office for 23 years, eventually qualifying as an architect and leaving to set up his own practice in Chandigarh.

The album Jaswinder Singh's father left him is a beautiful time capsule of that optimistic era. It ends abruptly with a final press cutting showing a picture of Le Corbusier wading into the sea, alongside a tribute to him by Hungarian-born architect Ernő Goldfinger: 'On Friday 27 August 1965 Le Corbusier died swimming in the Mediterranean.' (M.N. Sharma would later make a pilgrimage to Roquebrune-Cap-Martin in the South of France to visit Le Corbusier's beach cabin and grave.) Giani Rattan Singh died in 2006. Alongside a painting of the Golden Temple of Amritsar, one of the holiest sites in Sikhism, a niche in Jaswinder Singh's home contains a picture of his smiling father with a plaster relief sculpture he made of a bull – the hard-working animal which Le Corbusier identified with and liked to sketch – silhouetted against a bright blue sky.

The Secretariat Building by
Le Corbusier, 1953, with eggcrate
brise soleil

The Pump House on Sukhna Lake,
designed by Pierre Jeanneret with
a spiralling ramp

Jeet Malhotra

Jeet Malhotra, an architect and photographer, worked on the Chandigarh project from 1951 to 1966 in close collaboration with Le Corbusier, Pierre Jeanneret, Maxwell Fry and Jane Drew. He was Chief Architect of Punjab from 1981 to 1985 and then of the New Delhi Municipal Corporation from 1985 to 1987, when he also served as President of the Indian Council of Architecture. During his long career, he has designed numerous projects and evolved the concept of an 'Environmental Planning Unit' for the urban development of India.

I did not know what architecture was when in 1945, aged 15, I did my matriculation exams in the Urdu language in what was then Pakistan. By 1947, following independence and Partition, we had become refugees in our own country. My grandfather came from Pakistan, forcibly brought by the Indian army at the age of 100. When Nehru became prime minister, he appointed Koenigsberger as Director of Housing for the whole of India to help resettle refugees displaced by Partition. I went to the Delhi Polytechnic in Old Delhi where Otto Koenigsberger became my teacher. He came every week to the Department of Architecture and lectured us on town and country planning. We also had Indian teachers, but he became my guru.

Koenigsberger also had a private practice and very well-paid jobs planning the new capitals of Orissa, Bhubaneshwar and Gandhidham in Gujarat, near the border of Sindh. He appointed many people from America, engineers from Germany, people with a background in town and country planning. At the end of his lectures, he used to say: 'Gentlemen, boys, do you have any questions?' I used to put to him a lot of questions. He was very generous with his time, and eventually I went to see him looking for a job. He asked me if I knew anything about urban planning, and I replied: 'Only what you've taught me.' He told me that he would hire me, but that I wasn't to come into the office yet, but should go out into the city and find out for him what a neighbourhood unit was, and its ideal size.

At the time, I was living in Timarpur near Kingsway Camp, the largest refugee camp in Delhi. I studied the area thoroughly and after several days I was ready to write my report. Koenigsberger had told me not to write more than five points, and I brought some very expensive paper for a refugee and wrote five points in different colours. He shared it with all those who had come from outside India, so my standing with them went up. Koenigsberger then asked me to write a formal job application and say how much money I wanted. All I asked for was 375 rupees! This was in 1949 and I worked for him until 1951. I was very loyal to him. On the basis of my five points, he designed two cities. He was the first person to call me Jeet, which means Victory, and introduced me to such people as the Minister of the Health Department, describing me as a budding young architect from India.

Koenigsberger wanted houses to be made out of light, prefabricated material, but he failed in this and the factory houses fell apart. In the end, despite Nehru's support, he was sacked from his government job in 1951. In the meantime, the American architect Albert Mayer had been coming to Koenigsberger's office since 1949 to discuss plans for Chandigarh, a new city which would be the capital of Punjab, and I used to help correct the plans, so I knew what was cooking there. When the architect Matthew Nowicki who was working with him on the project died suddenly in an air crash in 1950, Mayer told Nehru that he couldn't finish the job without his best partner. That was how Le Corbusier and the others were brought in. After he was sacked, Koenigsberger, too, was trying to work on that capital project, but he had lots of bad publicity – the press was very strong, and they never spared anyone. So, I applied for a job with Le Corbusier's company.

The government was thinking of making the new capital mostly to rehabilitate refugees. An open competition was held to select the Indian architecture team, and people entered from all over the country. Entrants were asked to design a house with two rooms, a kitchen and a bathroom. Having worked for Koenigsberger for two to three years, I had becomes something of an expert in low-cost housing, so this was easy for me. Le Corbusier, Pierre Jeanneret, Maxwell Fry and Jane Drew came to inspect our work.

Only Fry and Drew spoke English, and they were also very good at French. Jeanneret was the quietest fellow in those days, but Le Corbusier was more aggressive and spoke some French, which Drew translated.

I asked Le Corbusier: 'What are you going to do, when everything has already been decided by Albert Mayer? So much work has been done – what are *you* going to do?' It put him in a very awkward position. Fry tried to defend the team. 'Are there no good architects in India able to do this?' I asked. 'Did you build the Taj Mahal here as Britishers? We have the finest architecture here in India.' Fry felt a little bit cheesed by this, but Drew was more agile; she told Le Corbusier and Fry: 'Here is this boy and we have heard his national pride – why don't you explain?' So, Fry talked about the Bauhaus, Le Corbusier's theories, and their work with climate architecture in Africa.

Finally, Le Corbusier stood up and said, 'I am a clean slate – I do not know what I will do there.' At Chandigarh everyone wanted to work with Fry and Drew, not Jeanneret, because they spoke English and no one understood French. So, I selected my own boss, Jeanneret, who was very small, very witty: I clicked with him. He made me and my wife a wooden table as a wedding present. Le Corbusier, when he came to India, did not want to work with me: 'I do not want to work with children,' he said. Le Corbusier wanted to employ more Europeans on the project, but P.N. Thapar, the first administrator of Chandigarh, wouldn't let him. Thapar was the only man Le Corbusier was scared of, because only he had the power to fire him.

I worked at Chandigarh until 1966. I was chief architect of Punjab from 1981 to 1985 and then of the New Delhi Municipal Corporation from 1985 to 1987, and I also served as president of the Indian Council of Architecture from 1984 to 1987. I want to open a university devoted to sustainability, so that we can have ideas for a future Chandigarh. Le Corbusier used to call for an open hand, which became the symbol of Chandigarh: what the world needs today is an open mind. No single man can solve the world's problems: we need a whole generation to evolve its own strategies. The answer is not Chandigarh. We have to think of a new Chandigarh for the next hundred years.

House Type 13-J (single storeyed),
Sector 22, Chandigarh, 1950s

The Open Hand Monument in the Capitol
Complex, designed by Le Corbusier
in 1954 and realized in 1985

'Africa

Beacons For

Must Unite

A Free Africa

or Perish!'

(Previous spread) Kwame Nkrumah
announcing Ghana's independence on
6 March 1957

Black Star Square in Accra, featuring a statue of
a soldier who symbolizes the West Africans who lost
their lives fighting for Ghana's independence

Independence Arch frames the sea in
Black Star Square, Accra, 1961

Henry Wellington

Henry Wellington was Head of the Department of Architecture at Kwame Nkrumah University of Science and Technology (KNUST), Kumasi, where he taught from 1972 to 2006 and was also a student. He then joined the Department of Archaeology and Heritage Studies, University of Ghana, Legon, and is currently engaged at the Ghana Heritage Committee as a Heritage Expert and a Cultural Heritage Activist. As a scholar, he has published extensively in the disciplines of architecture, urban design and cultural heritage.

In 1957, when Ghana's first Independence Day parade took place, I was among the schoolchildren who joined the procession in the colours of the new national flag – red, yellow and green with a black star. I wore a yellow jersey which my mother kept for many years. I don't know where it is now. The idea of Kwame Nkrumah standing there as the first president and parading in the colours of our own nation, not the Union Jack, affected me very deeply. I felt a great sense of patriotism. I got the impression that Nkrumah was a very visionary person.

Pan-Africanism, as I understand it, is very closely associated with Nkrumah. He went to the US, then to the UK, and came into contact with a number of Black African philosophers who were thinking about how Africa could reunite, and how the strength and the potential of Africa could be realized through this coming together. Nkrumah's thinking was that, in the desire for our self-actualization, we should see things in the context of Africa, not only the context of Ghana – it was too small for him. He was thinking that the potential of Ghana could only be reached if we were to see our strength in the totality of Africa.

Kwame Nkrumah University of Science and Technology (KNUST) was supposed to be, according to Nkrumah's dream, at the forefront of the nation's development of the nation. As a student, coming from Accra, I had been exposed to the colonial architecture – the old forts and castles, the traditional buildings – and I got to KNUST campus expecting a huge village. Wow! It was a city within the forest. I was amazed to see the new halls of residence. John Owusu Addo, who designed Unity Hall, had been to the Architectural Association (AA), so he had been exposed to the principles of Tropical Modernism. But because of his Ghanaian background, he had a good sense of history, too, and you can see the extent to which the sense of place was created and what I call the spirit of place was expressed. It was a fantastic experience for me to grow up in that environment.

From my perspective, we bought into the principles of Tropical Modernism, but we added to it the traditions we understood from traditional Ashanti architecture – the way in which the entrance loggia plays a very prominent role, for example, and the deep spiritual significance of Adinkra motifs to the psychology and sociology of the people. These are the things that no British architect – Jane Drew, Maxwell Fry, James Cubitt, Kenneth Scott, Denys Lasdun, none of them – took time to understand. A building from Ghana must show the evidence that it is Ghanaian because it's from within the context of Ghana. The people's culture, their economy, their circumstances and everything else must be reflected in the buildings.

My time at the School of Architecture coincided with the exchange programme with the Architectural Association, which brought John (Michael) Lloyd and teachers from the AA to Kumasi. And when I was in my second year, the whole faculty – staff and students – was sent to the AA for six weeks to participate in their activities. That was my first time ever going outside the country. At the AA, I could see that there was a very informal way of doing things – people were wearing loose shirts and had long hair at that time – but you could tell that these were very serious people doing creative work.

John Lloyd was young, with a spirit of adventure and a very passionate commitment to architectural education. There was a need for reform because KNUST students were not passing the foreign Royal Institute of British Architecture (RIBA) exams, where they had to learn about snow loads and other things that were not relevant to their experience. Lloyd restructured the entirety of KNUST, uniting the departments of building, planning and architecture into one faculty. Whereas there had previously been a course on the history of European architecture, there was now a lot of focus on the history of various cultures in Africa: we were studying the architecture of Egypt, Zimbabwe and Nigeria as well as Ghana. I personally was very deeply influenced by his idea that the school should go beyond mere architecture. I became a propagandist, I became a motivator, I became an initiator, I became an anthropologist.

Lloyd was able to organize world-famous architects to come and deliver very inspiring lectures. I remember Maxwell Fry's visit, and I remember the interaction we had as young students with these architects – especially with Jane Drew, a very lovely person, very kind and very passionate in her convictions about the need for Tropical Modernism. I remember Buckminster Fuller, who was a great source of inspiration for me as an individual. He showed us his design system for geodesic structures, which he explained you could use to cover the whole of the city of Accra using only a small amount of aluminium sheets, and we built examples on campus. Buckminster Fuller designed a huge geodesic structure for the International Trade Fair in Accra in 1967 and the various faculties and production centres of KNUST displayed their exhibitions under its dome.

I have great respect for the mind of Kwame Nkrumah. But what I disliked was the over-politicization of his ideas. His direction was faulty because he allowed himself to be influenced by a communist approach to public architecture and to be seduced by prestige buildings. For example, even the Trade Fair site – this huge African centre – has collapsed, because though the design was very prestigious, it was not sustainable. Nkrumah started very, very well but he went off the track. He began to become rather mean. For example, he passed the Preventive Detention Act, which allowed people to be incarcerated for no reason, just because they were in opposition.

People began to scheme to get him out, but because he had made the nation a one-party state there was no opposition and no political means to remove him from office. So, the military turned against him – with, as the history books tell us, the influence of the CIA. The great ideas Nkrumah had were not allowed to be brought to completion.

The School of Architecture and
Planning at KNUST, with a statue of a
female student holding a set square

The School of Engineering at KNUST
by James Cubitt and Partners, 1956

Commemorative cloth designed
for Independence Day
celebrations, 1957

Chapter  III

On 6 March 1957 Ghana became the first British colony in Africa to gain independence, and Kwame Nkrumah became the country's first prime minister. 'At long last the battle has ended!' Nkrumah shouted from his podium to the crowd who had assembled at midnight, in tribute to Nehru's independence speech of a decade before. 'And thus Ghana, your beloved country, is free for ever.'[1] Flanked by his colleagues, and visibly holding back tears, Nkrumah instructed the band to strike up Ghana's national anthem for the first time.

Ghana was the fourth Black state after Haiti, Liberia and Ethiopia to achieve independence. Celebrations in the newly independent country were the focus of international attention: over 600 reporters covered the five-day event, in which the Duchess of Kent (on behalf of the pregnant Queen Elizabeth II) and Governor General Sir Charles Arden-Clarke, dressed in court dress and ostrich plumes, formally transferred power to Ghana. Vice President Richard Nixon represented the United States and the Soviet delegation urged Nkrumah to visit Nikita Khrushchev with offers of 'fraternal assistance', as the Cold War superpowers vied for influence in Britain's place.[2]

Nkrumah, then 47, thought that the independence of Ghana was meaningless unless it was the spearhead for the liberation of all Africa. (He later put it with more urgency: 'Africa must unite or perish!')[3] He offered full-throated support and financial assistance to the freedom struggles of other colonized countries in Africa, and in 1958 lent newly independent Guinea £10m, hoping that the resulting Ghana-Guinea coalition would be the start of a Union of African States. Over the next decade the so-called 'winds of change', in Harold Macmillan's famous phrase, would sweep across Africa and 32 countries – two-thirds of the continent – won independence.[4] 'It is clear that we must find an African Solution to our problems, and this can only be found in African Unity,' Nkrumah insisted. 'Divided we are weak. United Africa could become one of the greatest forces for good in the world.'[5]

Ghana's independence came only a couple of months after the Montgomery bus boycott, a turning point in the Civil Rights campaign in America, and Martin Luther King and his wife Coretta Scott King were in the audience for Nkrumah's speech.

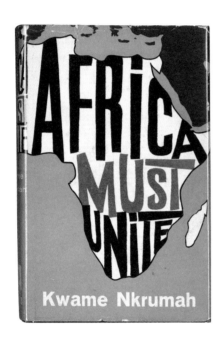

Africa Must Unite by
Kwame Nkrumah, 1964

Ghana President Kwame Nkrumah, whom Cassius calls "my personal hero," leads champ and his (Cassius') "kid brother" Rahaman Ali (alias Rudolph Clay) on tour of Flagstaff House, official presidential residence in Accra. Ghana officials follow trio.

Nkrumah on the cover of *Drum*, 1957

Nkrumah with Muhammad Ali dressed in *kente* in *Ebony*, 1964

A passionate Pan-Africanist, Nkrumah encouraged the diaspora uprooted by the transatlantic slave trade to return and help rebuild what he hoped might be a United States of Africa – a Pan-African federation of which he presumed he would be the first president. W.E.B. Du Bois and George Padmore, the founding fathers of Pan-Africanism, moved to Ghana, while prominent figures such as activist Malcolm X, poet Maya Angelou and boxer Muhammad Ali made much-publicized pilgrimages to the country. *Ebony* magazine devoted nine pages to Ali's 1964 trip to Africa: he was photographed wearing *kente* – a Ghanaian textile made of narrow strips of handwoven silk and cotton cloth – as he was driven through the streets of Accra in a convertible, as well as next to his 'personal hero' Nkrumah. It was reported that 'Ali loved Africa, and Africa loved him', and he was gifted four plots of land in the hope that he would make Ghana his permanent home.[6]

Nkrumah wanted to restore the pride in indigenous culture that he felt had been repressed by colonialism, and proudly wore Ghanaian traditional dress on the world stage. He wore *kente* on formal occasions, such as the opening of Parliament and on his visits to meet President Eisenhower at the White House, and a *fugu* smock from the Northern Region – his battledress – when announcing the country's independence. His use of traditional attire from tribes not his own (the Nzima) served to unite Ghana's different ethnic groups, and was seen as an intrinsic part of the decolonizing process.

In 1958 Ghana hosted the first All-African Peoples' Conference at Maxwell Fry and Jane Drew's Community Centre; this was the first Pan-African gathering on the continent. Nkrumah took to the stage under the slogans 'Hands off Africa!', 'Africa Must Be Free!' and 'Down with Imperialism and Colonialism!' and argued for a Pan-African federation that would unite the continent and help forge a new post-colonial African identity. 'We want to develop our own community and an African personality,' he said. 'Others may feel that they have evolved the very best way of life, but we are not bound, like slavish imitators, to accept it as our mould … If we find the methods used by others are suitable to our social environments, we shall adopt them; if we find them unsuitable, we shall reject them.'[7]

The All-African People's
Conference at the Community
Centre, Accra, 1958

Nkrumah saw Ghanaian art forms, dismissed as 'primitive' by Europeans (though given new value in ethnographic museums in the West), as important assets both for national development and for the creation of a modern Pan-African cultural identity. He urged Africans to rediscover and celebrate their heritage, commissioning the composer J.H. Kwabena Nketia to create a cultural policy for Ghana and inviting Drew and Fry to design a National Museum in Accra to showcase Ghana's history and this African Renaissance. With their architectural partner Denys Lasdun, Drew and Fry created a low, sleek building that had an eye-shaped plan, glass louvres on every façade and a rotunda that flooded the space with natural light. The striking aluminium roof was based on the Dome of Discovery at the 1951 Festival of Britain. Inside this metal dome and around a mezzanine were objects representing and symbolically integrating all the competing ethnic groups of the new Ghana. These were shown alongside artefacts from across Africa to assert Nkrumah's continental ambitions. The museum was opened by the Duchess of Kent as part of the 1957 Independence Day celebrations.

Despite Tropical Modernism's colonial associations – with Fry and Drew creating what was effectively a late imperial style in the Gold Coast – Tropical Modernism survived the transition because Nkrumah saw in this architecture not only the possibility for nation-building, symbolizing the progressiveness and internationalism of the new Ghana, but an expression of his Pan-African ideology. Fry and Drew continued to work in Ghana and, taking advantage of the optimistic mood around independence, Nkrumah also invited Ghanaian architects back from America to create cutting-edge designs for modern Ghana. Among those he persuaded to return was Victor Adegbite, who had trained in architecture at Howard University and studied housing in Jamaica and Puerto Rico. Essentially becoming the government's chief architect, Adegbite headed the Housing Corporation and then the Ghana National Construction Company (GNCC), which was responsible for all large government projects. He was the driving force behind the establishment of the Ghana Institute of Architects in 1962 and helped establish a new architecture school at Kwame Nkrumah University of Science and Technology (KNUST).

National Museum of Ghana by Fry, Drew, Drake and Lasdun, Accra, 1957

Victor Adegbite in 1963

Nkrumah dancing with Queen
Elizabeth II in Accra, 1961

Adegbite shared Nkrumah's vision for Africa and led several monumental projects such as Black Star Square, built on the old colonial polo grounds in Accra, to commemorate Ghana becoming a republic (and Nkrumah its first president) in July 1960. A triumphal gate capped with a black star, to symbolize African freedom, stood on the square, and another huge triple arch framed the sea. This was intended as a door of return, the opposite of the 'door of no return' in the colonial forts through which so many Africans were forced as part of the transatlantic slave trade: a beacon for the free and united Africa to which Nkrumah hoped to attract the diaspora back. Tropical Modernism was adapted to create a uniquely African form of expression. Queen Elizabeth II (having by now given birth) attended the 1961 celebrations, at which she famously danced with Nkrumah and persuaded him to keep Ghana in the Commonwealth. On the balcony of the arch, overlooking the square from under a huge umbrella – a symbol of chiefly power – Nkrumah sat alongside Ghana's former queen and watched the independence celebrations. His powers considerably increased, he was symbolically positioned as the leader of the United States of Africa for which he hoped.

Before the Queen's visit, the bronze statue of Nkrumah by Italian sculptor Nicola Cataudella, positioned in front of Parliament House, had been bombed. The statue showed Nkrumah striding forward in *fugu* dress with his arm raised ('Forward Ever! Backwards Never!' was the slogan of his political party). Nkrumah's self-aggrandizing gestures – he had begun to style himself Osagyefo, the 'redeemer', encouraging his hero worship as the 'Founder of the Nation' – annoyed his political opponents and, as well as the bombing of his statue, there was the first of several assassination attempts.[8]

Nonetheless, Nkrumah's portrait, and the Modernist buildings he commissioned, replaced the face of the Queen on money and stamps as a clear signal of the transfer of power. He explained in a British newspaper that he was not 'power-drunk with success' or planning 'sedition against the Queen', but had included his portrait 'because many of my people cannot read or write' and had to be 'shown that they are now really independent. And they can only be shown by signs.'[9]

Black Star Square, Accra, built on
the former colonial playing fields
for state celebrations, 1957

Independence Arch and Black Star Gate,
completed in 1961 in time for the state
visit of Queen Elizabeth II to Ghana

A shop assistant at the Sick-Hagemeyer store in Accra photographed by James Barnor, 1971

Northern Territories chiefs with a model of the Volta River Project, 1950–4

Architecture was one of these signs, a key symbol of Ghana's newfound independence, and Modernist buildings appeared prominently on postcards and record covers in the 1950s and '60s, alongside touristic images of shoppers in Accra's colourful markets and musicians in traditional dress. Ghana's new architecture also formed the cosmopolitan backdrop for photographs depicting the latest fashions, including those by James Barnor, a photojournalist with a studio, Ever Young, in the Jamestown district of Accra. Barnor recorded the journey to independence and Ghana's changing cityscape for the city's *Daily Graphic* newspaper as well as the influential South African magazine *Drum*. In these publications, Nkrumah was often presented as 'the Architect of the New Ghana'.[10] Tropical Modernism was how Ghana wanted to present itself not only to its own inhabitants but to the rest of the world.[9]

The shining dome of the National Museum had been made from bauxite mined in Ghana but processed into aluminium in Britain, which then exported the finished panels back to Ghana. Nkrumah smarted at the fact that the colonists had exploited the country's mineral resources in this way but spent all their profits abroad. He now wanted to oblige foreign companies to invest in factories and to produce goods in Ghana. Nkrumah had an ambitious plan to dam the Volta River, which would create the largest man-made lake in the world, and to use the resulting hydroelectric energy to power a smelting plant to be run by the new Volta Aluminium Company. A travelling exhibition of cinema vans toured the country and screened propagandistic animations aimed at selling voters on the expensive scheme. The dam was controversial, too, as it required the rehousing of 77,000 people, but Nkrumah hoped it would be a flagship for Ghana's ambitious industrial and social strategy.

By the 1950s, international trade had outstripped the capacities of Ghana's ports and Tema, the new harbour city Nkrumah commissioned 32km east of Accra, was chosen as the site of Ghana's new aluminium smelting plant. The Volta-Tema scheme was modelled on Nehru's Bhakra Nangal Dam and Chandigarh, construction sites that Nkrumah visited in December 1958 – a

Ghana Rhythm, highlife
record, 1957

Members of the Uhuru Dance Band
wearing *fugu*, 1963

tour on which Nkrumah had been greeted, Bombay's *Free Press Journal* noted, as the 'African Mahatma' (Gandhi). Nkrumah's British secretary Erica Powell recalled that as she and Nkrumah admired the Bhakra Dam, they trailed 'up and down the most terrifying rough wooden steps and scaffolding that overhung deep ravines'.[11] To inspect the structure, which used 3.5 million cubic metres of concrete and stretched half a kilometre across a steep Himalayan gorge, Nkrumah wore a black velour coat that Nehru had given him in Delhi to protect against the chilly cold. That afternoon, his party went to see Chandigarh, also a building site, with the Secretariat building only recently finished. Nehru liked to showcase Chandigarh to other non-aligned leaders as a potential model for their own future cities. 'It seemed to me like suddenly landing on another planet,' Powell remarked. 'There was not the slightest feeling of India in those futuristic designs.'[12]

Echoing Nehru's 'temples of modern India' speech, Nkrumah described projects such as the Volta Dam as 'the new "places of Pilgrimage" in this modern Age of Science and Technology. They serve as monuments to the determination and dedication of a whole people to raise themselves to a fuller and richer life.'[13] Just as Nehru hoped to unite a multi-faith India behind a secular constitution and his industrial schemes, Nkrumah hoped to bring together the many ethnic groups that made up Ghana under his Soviet-inspired notion of African Socialism. He acknowledged his debt to the 'inspiration' of Gandhi and the 'superhuman efforts' of Nehru, whose books he had read as a student and with whose view that modernization and industrialization were the key to national self-sufficiency he concurred.[14] 'What other countries have taken three hundred years or more to achieve,' Nkrumah asserted, 'a once dependent territory must try to accomplish in a generation if it is to survive. Unless it is, as it were, "jet-propelled", it will lag behind and thus risk everything for which it has fought.'[15]

Ghana and India were founding members of the Non-Aligned Movement, which was formed in 1955 at the Afro-Asian conference in Bandung, Indonesia. Both countries adopted a policy of neutralism, refusing to take sides in the Cold War between the USA and Soviet Union. By 1961, when the movement was formalized with 53 members, the neutralist group was bigger than both Cold

Postcards showing Tropical Modernism as a
symbol of the new Ghana, 1959-73

Clockwise from top left: Republic Hall at
KNUST, Kumasi; Central Library, Independence
Arch, Black Star Gate and Bank of Ghana, Accra

132

Ghana House - Accra

Clockwise from top left: Kingsway Store, Ambassador
Hotel, Standard Bank of West Africa, Ghana House
(Leventis Building) and a street scene, Accra

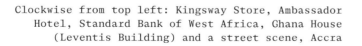

Flats and CEO housing designed by Fry, Drew, Drake and Lasdun in Tema, 1950–9

War powers. It argued for decolonization, disarmament and a new world order that would break imperial patterns of cultural and economic dominance by the Global North (Le Corbusier designed an open hand for Nehru as the symbol of this peaceful ideal; when it went unused, he recycled it as the logo for Chandigarh). Ghana, Nkrumah asserted, would 'seek advice and help from all; but dictation and direction from none'.[16]

He was therefore able to secure funding from both power blocs, playing them off against each other as they eagerly competed for political influence in post-colonial Africa. The Volta Dam would be Nkrumah's most expensive infrastructure project, shifting perceptions about Africa's underdevelopment, and required a major international consortium of funders, predominantly from Britain and America, as well as the World Bank (Nkrumah simultaneously pursued funding from the Soviet Union and China to realize the Bui Dam on the Black Volta). There was a debate in Nkrumah's administration as to whether these mega-projects would help Ghana transcend neo-colonial dependencies or perpetuate what Nehru had called the 'whirlpool of economic imperialism'.[17]

Nkrumah showed such personal interest in the Tema project that it was thought that plans were afoot to make this 'first-class modern city', without the 'legacies of the past to hamper its development', Ghana's new post-colonial capital.[18] Its Tropical Modernist design was an important symbol of the new state. Accra, however, remained the seat of power, and Nkrumah also invested in Modernist schemes in the capital (such as a new airport, Korle Bu Hospital and the Ambassador Hotel), transforming its skyline in the process. Just as the independent Indian administration had taken over Lutyens's Delhi, Nkrumah took up residence in the former Governor of the Gold Coast's official residence, Osu Castle. This had been a point of transit for enslaved Africans, and Nkrumah was conscious of the symbolic importance of his choice. The Public Works Department added government offices in the Tropical Modernist style in an internal courtyard of the Danish-built fort.

Nkrumah appointed his close friend Theodore Shealtiel Clerk, with whom he had been to Achimota School, to head the newly founded Tema Development Corporation (TDC) and lead the team of largely British architects designing Tema. Clerk had graduated in architecture from the University of Edinburgh, where he went on a Commonwealth scholarship, returning to the Gold Coast in 1946 as the country's only professionally qualified architect. In 1962 he became the first president of the Ghana Institute of Architects, the professional body that replaced the Gold Coast Society of Architects, a social club established in the colonial era. The TDC was conceived as a kind of 'live school' like that at Chandigarh, with a team of 16 European architects and planners working alongside several hundred African employees. It was also a research centre where new construction methods were tested and implemented.

Michael Hirst was one of three architects recruited from the Department of Tropical Architecture at the Architectural Association (AA) to work on Tema, having turned down the opportunity to work with Minnette de Silva in Sri Lanka (Kenneth Frampton, who became a theorist of Critical Regionalism, was to be a fourth but he went to the US instead). In 1956 he travelled to Ghana for his first 18-month 'tour'. In his current canal-side home in a suburb of London, Hirst still holds a box of plans, drawn up by the British architect Alfred 'Bunny' Alcock along the lines of Harlow and other British New Towns. Hirst's many construction photographs of the nascent city record the high-end CEO houses, built for captains of industry, that would bring employment to Tema, as well as the stylish Tropical Modernist apartment blocks designed by Fry and Drew and their partners Lindsay Drake and Denys Lasdun under Clerk's supervision. Hirst and his wife Mary, who was employed as one of Nkrumah's secretaries helping to draft Ghana's new constitution, moved from Accra to live in one of these apartments as they helped build the rest of the city.

Tema was planned initially for 85,000 people and the team developed, as architectural scholar Iain Jackson puts it, a confident lexicon of 'exposed concrete, decorative screens and large interlocking geometric forms'.[19] Buildings with monopitch roofs were long and thin, and fitted with glass and aluminium louvres to take advantage of prevailing sea breezes. Drew worked on Tema Manhean, the resettlement of the *Ga* fishing village that the city displaced, and Fry built 'labour lines' and ablution blocks for the large number of workers devoted to the project. As at Chandigarh, as Hirst explains, 'women formed a major part of the workforce; they carried concrete in head-pans from the mixers to the men doing the pouring of footing or slabs, or they carried concrete blocks on their heads to wherever required.'[20] They also, he noticed, co-designed the settlement, adapting the floorplans of their houses, which avoided traditional courtyard forms, to the requirements of their mixed households.

With the Ghanaian team, Hirst built four colourful Independence Day parade floats which were modelled on those he had made as a student for AA carnivals. Constructed on the backs of trucks out of chicken wire and papier-mâché, they show large models of Tema and its new port as symbols of modern Ghana. Teetering portrayals of Fry, Drew and Partners' apartment blocks, seeming to emerge as if from surf, are rendered in the same bright colours as Ghana's new national flag. Hirst and his European colleagues waved off the flotilla as it left Tema for the capital: 'As Independence was very much an African affair, we stayed away from the actual celebration, just in case the participants got over-excited,' he wrote in a memoir. 'On the following day a huge Durbar was staged in Achimota, when the tribal chiefs from all over Ghana were assembled and presented to the Duchess, complete with the Royal Marines bands and African Horseguards on parade.'[21]

In 1960, having just returned from Chandigarh, Nkrumah hired the Greek planner Constantinos Doxiadis to work on Tema. Doxiadis was then planning Islamabad (the new capital of Pakistan) and a scheme for an Africa-wide road system in which Nkrumah, unsurprisingly, showed much interest. Doxiadis was very critical of the British scheme by Alcock, with its winding paths and 'disorganised' and 'haphazard' plan; he proposed an ambitious new masterplan that considered Tema with Accra and the Volta Delta as part of an enormous urban region.[22] He redesigned Tema along a rigorous mathematical system with a plan that used a grid of main roads to delineate 19 neighbourhood communities of various income groups, reminiscent of Le Corbusier's radical grid scheme for Chandigarh. It was a rationalist, visionary plan that

Independence Day floats
featuring Tema, 1957

appealed to Nkrumah and his ambitions for Ghana – in short, it was his Chandigarh.

With the Fry, Drew and Partners projects complete, the TDC stopped employing British consultants, worried about their continued influence. A deal to produce prefabricated elements in a factory imported from the USSR was done with the Soviets, but it never came to fruition; in the meantime all the architectural work and experimental homes built at Tema were delivered by Clerk and his small team of African architects and engineers.

★

In 1964 Kwame Nkrumah asked Victor Adegbite to design a complex for the Organisation of African Unity Conference, due to be held in Accra the following year. Nkrumah thought it important that it was designed with local talent and expertise; he sketched out initial plans on a napkin, and Adegbite designed the complex and supervised the team that constructed it on a tight deadline. Having drafted a constitution for a Union of African States, Nkrumah hoped to use the conference to encourage wavering nations such as Nigeria, Ethiopia and Liberia to support his idea of political as well as economic unity. He thought the complex might be the future headquarters of this United States of Africa, but his rivals were suspicious of his intentions to lead it.

Adegbite's structure – known as Job 600, as it was the 600th project under the supervision of the Ghana Public Works Department – was hugely expensive. The 12-storey building, which contained conference and banqueting halls, executive suites and a roof garden, was finished in 10 months, with construction teams working around the clock. Any foreign architectural contribution was underplayed, with the local newspapers reporting that the furniture and furnishings were all produced in Ghana, a symbol of pride in the new African vision.

Under Nkrumah's indigenization or Africanization policy, Ghanaian architects were required partners on all construction projects, and as well as Tema they worked on a spate of school, hospital and infrastructure projects all over Ghana. Often, local architects worked alongside those Nkrumah commissioned from other non-aligned countries, such as Yugoslavia (with which Ghana began a foreign-relations programme) and other countries

Job 600 built for the
Organisation of African Unity
Conference, 1965

in the Eastern Bloc, as well as Israel, the Soviet Union and China. As an important part of his Africanization policy – and because the few Black architects there were in Ghana had all trained abroad – in 1964 a training programme between KNUST in Kumasi and the AA in London was set up.

The AA had founded a Tropical School in London a decade earlier. As its first director, Maxwell Fry had been tasked with training students for work in Britain's colonies by drilling them in the climatic principles of Tropical Modernism. At first the students were mostly from the United Kingdom, being readied for lucrative work in Britain's colonies, but increasingly – as can be seen in the huge leather-bound roll in the AA archive – students arrived from post-colonial countries in the Commonwealth. By this time Koenigsberger – who, like Fry, had worked in India and Ghana – was director of the programme, having renamed it the Department of Tropical Studies in 1961 to reflect a new focus on scientific research, social housing and planning. Even then, the curriculum still retained a western bias that reflected the late colonial origins of Tropical Modernism, and its universalist, centralized approach failed to address specific cultures and conditions. The engagement with KNUST, 'practically a branch of the Architectural Association school in West Africa' according to Koenigsberger, would call into question and force the re-evaluation of these metropolitan assumptions.[23]

In 1964 the AA sent John (Michael) Lloyd, a first-year tutor with no previous experience of the Tropics, to KNUST to head a new Department of Architecture which had 39 staff, including several sent from the Department of Tropical Architecture, and 271 students, some of whom were exchanged in both directions. The first architecture school south of the Sahara, KNUST is sometimes referred to as a 'Bauhaus in the Tropics'.[24] Its large campus in the tropical rainforest near Kumasi had begun with a few prefabricated huts in 1952, dilapidated photographs of which were contrasted in the Ghanaian press ('what Britain thought fit for the African') with the new developments at Tema and elsewhere.[25] The campus now features numerous experimental Tropical Modernist buildings by British architects such as James Cubitt and Kenneth Scott and Yugoslavian architects including

John (Michael) Lloyd with KNUST students on a fieldtrip to London, 1964

Miro Marasović and Niksa Ciko, as well as Ghanaian architects such as John Owusu Addo and Samuel Opare Larbi, both of whom were sent to London to study at the Tropical School.

At first KNUST did not have a school of architecture, but it was encouraged to create one in a UN report co-authored by Koenigsberger. It accepted its first students in 1958. Anthony Chitty, who had been to the AA (before working for the Russian émigré architect Berthold Lubetkin's architectural collective Tecton), was on the governing council and gave the opening address, 'A Ghanaian Aesthetic?', in which he asked:

> Is a regional architecture, a truly African style, possible for West Africa; for Ghana in particular? I believe the answer to this question is 'yes': not only possible but desirable, something to be striven for ... Not just a pallid and mediocre edition of the international style, not just the half considered European solution trotted out to make do here, but a real and living architectural answer to your own local problems, social, technical and political, drawing the maximum from such origins as do exist here, a true Ghana aesthetic.[26]

Lloyd invited leading figures in Tropical Architecture to KNUST as guest teachers, including Jane Drew and Otto Koenigsberger, as well as lecturers from the US, Czechoslovakia, Hungary, Pakistan, Poland, West Germany and Yugoslavia. Other international luminaries included the utopian architect Buckminster Fuller, who visited the school for three weeks in 1964 to discuss the role architects might play in the future success of mankind. Students made a series of geodesic domes under his supervision, including several 6m-high (20ft) models made of bamboo and covered in mud, which Fuller thought would solve the housing problems in the Volta region. 'Fuller was perhaps the most one-track man I ever knew,' recalled Drew of their time together at KNUST. 'The most enthusiastic and verbose. He really believed that his engineering inventions could change the world, economise the use of material and beat the climate.'[27] When shown his mud domes, Drew pointed out that, unless he could stabilize the earth, they

Buckminster Fuller admiring a dome while teaching at KNUST, 1964

Students and faculty working on a Buckminster Fuller-inspired geodesic structure, 1964

COMMUNITY
BUILDING IN
THE UPPER
REGION OF
GHANA

KUMASI STUDY

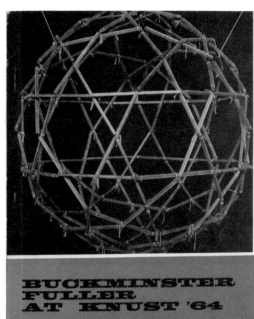

BUCKMINSTER
FULLER
AT KNUST '64

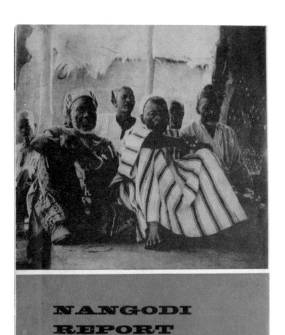

NANGODI
REPORT

Reports and studies by the
Department of Architecture,
KNUST, 1960s

would be destroyed in the first rain. Researchers visiting Kumasi in 2023 discovered a surviving aluminium dome, 1.8m (6ft) in diameter, buried under a pile of wood in a storeroom at the University's engineering workshop, a hangar-like building sometimes attributed to Fuller.

Whereas Fry and Drew had seen little to learn from traditional African architecture, Lloyd showed a new appreciation of cultural as well as climatic context and instituted a new course covering the History of Cultures, with a special focus on African architecture, treated as equal to European creations. These classes broke down some of the western assumptions about vernacular architecture perpetuated by the Department of Tropical Architecture and helped advocate for a new regionalism. The relationship with the AA had been founded after KNUST students had for two years running failed their Royal Institute of British Architects (RIBA) exams; this accreditation seemed to be a continuation of the colonial past, and it was decided that a new curriculum appropriate to the specific needs and conditions of Ghana was required. Lloyd argued that if KNUST was 'to truly contribute to the future of the continent, [it] must drastically define anew the task of "architect"'.[28] He hired Ghanaian teachers such as John Owusu Addo, who had graduated in 1957 from the Regent Street Polytechnic in London (now the University of Westminster) and who was sent to the AA for postgraduate training at the Tropical School, and J. Max Bond Jr., an African American architect who had trained at Harvard University and came to Ghana at Nkrumah's invitation.

Addo constructed many of the buildings on campus and, with Bond, led students including Samuel Larbi, Daniel Sydney Kpodo-Tay and Henry Wellington on trips into the rural regions around the new Volta Dam to learn from indigenous architecture and plan resettlement projects. In an edition of *Arena* devoted to the Kumasi school, Addo and Bond argued that post-colonial architects 'must assume a broader place in society, as consolidators, innovators, propogandists, activists, as well as designers'.[29] They self-consciously adapted Tropical Modernism to incorporate traditional Ghanaian elements – not to imitate the past but to create a new fusion for the future.

J. Max Bond Jr. on right, 1960s

Bolgatanga Library designed by J. Max
Bond Jr. for the Ghana National
Construction Corporation, 1965

Patrick Wakely's prototype of a
classroom, Madina, Accra, 1967

Addo, for example, served as chief architect for several of KNUST's campus buildings, including the Senior Staff Clubhouse with the Yugoslavian architect Miro Marasović, a square glass building elevated on slender pillars or pilotis, with a wrap-around veranda and wooden louvres to shield the large open-plan interior space from the heat. In a courtyard space was a circular dance floor situated over a reflective pool, where the faculty would jive to highlife, a musical genre combining African metre and jazz melodies that Nkrumah promoted as Ghana's national music. Ghanaian bandleader E.T. Mensah, who composed the independence song 'Ghana Freedom', described highlife as 'indigenous music played on foreign instruments'.[30] Similarly, Ghana's architects fused the traditional with the modern as they contributed to shaping a new identity for Ghana and Africa.

Speaking in 2023 from the house he designed for himself in Kumasi, the 95-year-old Addo recalled of the Club House that it was 'very, very, very successful, busy at lunchtime and very busy at night. It was a joy to be there.'[31] In the early 1960s, Addo also designed Unity Hall with Marasović. Loosely inspired by Le Corbusier's Unité d'habitation in Marseille, it is composed of two nine-storey blocks, elevated on large columns, that have a double banked row of 448 rooms, each with a balcony (because Addo knew Ghanaian students would prefer to be outside whenever possible) and a corridor between that is open to the breeze. A lower, linking block creates a courtyard between the larger buildings and contains the refectory, with a kitchen in the basement below – an arrangement that Addo recalls was inspired by the restaurants he'd been to along Oxford Street in London. In 1969 Addo became Unity Hall's first master and in 1974 he replaced Lloyd as the first Black head of the Department of Architecture.

As his student Henry Wellington explains, Addo 'had been to [the AA], so he was exposed to the principles of Tropical Modernism. But because of his Ghanaian background, he has a good sense of history, too, and you can see the extent to which the sense of place was created and what I call the spirit of place was expressed.'[32] Wellington, who came from Accra, remembers being amazed when he first arrived on campus to see these towering new halls of residence in the rainforest and points out the significance of their having been designed by an African architect: 'From my perspective, we bought into the principles of Tropical Modernism but we added to it the traditions we understood from traditional Ashanti architecture, for example, the way in which the entrance loggia plays a very prominent role, and the deep spiritual significance of Adinkra motifs to the psychology and sociology of the people.' These, Wellington notes, were things that none of the British architects took the time to understand.

African American architect J. Max Bond Jr. was also invited back to Ghana by Nkrumah and worked there from 1964 to 1967. The community library he designed in the northern town of Bolgatanga while at KNUST shows the renewed interest the university's tutors fostered in vernacular architecture, and is an essay on the ways in which this can be combined with the principles of Tropical Modernism. Inspired by local courtyard housing and the Frafra architecture of North East Ghana – buildings that are highly decorated with bold, geometric patterns – Bond included four structures, each with a different function, unified under a raised concrete roof designed to provide shade and encourage air circulation. Bond, who also designed the Studio and Practice Hall for the National Orchestra in Accra, considered his work for the Ghana Library Board to be his first independent work and it was his most significant Ghanaian project, a skilful African take on Tropical Modernism.

Patrick Wakely, who joined the KNUST faculty from the Department of Tropical Architecture, explains that he and his white colleagues were there not to impose an architecture, as the colonialists had done, 'but to engage people and respond to their ambitions, and to enable them to achieve them through design expertise or technical understandings'.[33] He originally signed up to go to Ghana for idealistic reasons, 'because of my admiration for Kwame Nkrumah and his concept of Pan-Africanism, post-colonialism and the non-aligned movement. That came across very clearly when I read his book *Consciencism,* which caught the attention and the support and the solidarity of many of us.' But already cracks were starting to appear. Wakeley remembers the suspicion that some of the students, who had attended the Kwame Nkrumah Ideological Institute at Winneba, were on the staff at the prime ministerial home Flagstaff House, spies planted at KNUST to make sure that its teachers and students were not a threat to the state.

KNUST became something of an architectural laboratory for Nkrumah's vision for Ghana and the continent. In 1966 KNUST students, still inspired by Fuller's visit, created a large dome for the first International Trade Fair site, which was located between Accra and Tema. The dome housed examples of student work, all aimed at assisting in what Lloyd called 'the self-transformation of Africa'.[34] The International Trade Fair was one of Nkrumah's most ambitious projects, showcasing Ghana's mineral wealth and investment opportunities to a global audience. Designed according to the principles of Tropical Modernism by Polish architects Jacek Chyrosz and Stanisław Rymaszewski, under the direction of Victor Adegbite, the new site was studded with pavilions and stands. Its centrepiece was the Africa Pavilion, a huge circular building open to the sea breeze with an aluminium roof to provide shade and protect against rain, its design inspired by the royal umbrellas of the Akan chiefs.

On 24 February 1966, however, just before the Trade Fair was due to open, and as Nkrumah was en route to Hanoi at the invitation of Ho Chi Minh on a peace mission to resolve the Vietnam war, he was ousted in a military coup. Nkrumah had made Ghana a one-party state and installed himself as president for life, imprisoning his opponents without trial, and there was no political route to deposing him. The International Trade Fair was finally inaugurated in 1967, on the anniversary of the coup, by Joseph Arthur Ankrah, the army general who had deposed and succeeded Nkrumah. Today the site lies deserted and decayed. A faded sign memorializes a Pan-African bookshop, long gone. The aluminium roof of the Africa Pavilion was ripped off by a storm some years ago, and the geodesic dome built by KNUST students was similarly blown away.

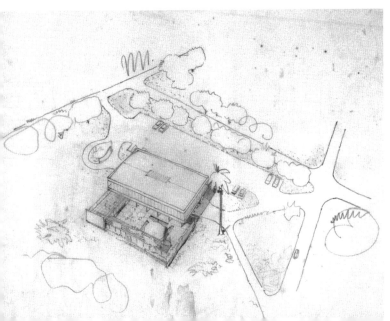

(Left) Senior Staff Clubhouse designed
by John Owusu Addo at KNUST
(Above and right) Unity Hall by
John Owusu Addo and Miro Marasović at
KNUST, 1965

Africa Hall by John Owusu Addo
and Nikso Ciko, KNUST, 1967

Unity Hall by John Owusu Addo and
Miro Marasović, KNUST, 1967

John Owusu Addo

John Owusu Addo was the first Ghanaian Professor of Architecture at Kwame Nkrumah University of Science and Technology (KNUST) in Kumasi, where he served for most of his career in several capacities, including Chief University Architect, Dean of the Faculty of Architecture and Pro-Vice-Chancellor. A graduate of the Regent Street Polytechnic (now the University of Westminster), in 1964 he obtained a Postgraduate Certificate in Tropical Architecture from the Architectural Association School of Architecture, London. In 2007 he was presented with the Ghana Institute of Architect's Life-time Achievement Award.

Before independence there wasn't much of what we would call modern architecture in Ghana. Having won a scholarship that I saw advertised in the *Gold Coast Gazette*, I trained in architecture at the Regent Street Polytechnic in London (now the University of Westminster), graduating in 1958. I then came back home. After working with Kenneth Scott for two years I was invited to join the architects at the Kwame Nkrumah University of Science and Technology (KNUST) in Kumasi; some of the English lads were going away and they wanted a Ghanaian to participate in the development of the campus. I thought I would stay only about two to three years then go back to set up a practice in Accra. But I was given the opportunity to design, which is what every young architect wants to do – I mean, I don't see in which other organization I would have been given the chance to design a Senior Staff Clubhouse or a hall of residence. So, I felt that this was my place.

The Senior Staff Clubhouse was the Vice-Chancellor's idea. He wanted to see a very busy place. He didn't want people to move from room to room. When you got there, you'd see people playing table tennis, billiards – everything was open. I tell you, it was very, very, very successful – busy at lunchtime and very busy at night. It was a joy to be there. I designed Unity Hall with the Yugoslavian architect Miro Marasović, brought in by an arrangement between President Tito and President Nkrumah. It has a double banked row of rooms with a corridor in between, open at each end, with aluminium shutters that allowed for a breeze through the rooms. We orientated the building in such a way that the broadsides faced the cooler north and south, and it has balconies that provided shading and which the students enjoyed.

The architecture course had been started here in Kumasi in about 1958. They were doing a Royal Institute of British Architects (RIBA) syllabus and the Vice-Chancellor of the University felt that was not the right thing to do – the course needed to be geared to the needs of Ghana and the Tropics. So, he invited John (Michael) Lloyd to bring his ideas from the Architectural Association (AA). Lloyd devised this new faculty structure, and because I had done a few buildings on campus it put me in very good light, and Lloyd straightaway told the Vice-Chancellor that he wanted me to join the faculty. To do that, I first had to go to the AA to do the Tropical Architecture course under Otto Koenigsberger, to learn about sunshading and the best way to position buildings in the humid Tropics. Koenigsberger, who was German by birth but Indian by naturalization, had a lot of experience in the Tropics, and had been part of the UN development programme that initiated the first designs for the port city of Tema in Ghana.

I met Jane Drew at the AA where she often joined reviews of student work. She was a chain-smoker and a very good critic. I also went to Maxwell Fry's lectures. I didn't know it then, but I discovered that some years earlier when I attended Wesley (Teacher Training) College in Kumasi, I had lived in one of their distinctive, modern buildings. Their architecture was very practical, very exciting, and tried to answer the needs of the hot and humid Tropics. Now architects are just copying these glass boxes which are dependent on air conditioning and even then you're not comfortable inside – it's a trend that I think should not be encouraged. I think we should make use of Fry and Drew's scientific methods for providing shade and cooling.

There were six Ghanaians on the Tropical Architecture course, two Nigerians, as well as students from Afghanistan, Chile and Honduras. It was very international. I had no difficulty as a Black student – no difficulty at all – my classmates were very friendly with me. After graduating, a few of us bought an old English taxi and toured Europe visiting all the cathedrals, churches and chateaux. And then I came back to KNUST to teach.

Lloyd was very concerned that our teaching should reflect African culture. Students spent two weeks conducting surveys and community projects, observing and studying life in rural villages and towns, and then making proposals as to how to redesign them. He renamed the History of Architecture course the History of Cultures. Students no longer just learned about St Peter's Basilica and Borromini in Florence, or any other of these big architectural set pieces in Europe, but also about the mosques of northern Ghana and other African architecture. Jane Drew and Maxwell Fry and the others would come in to teach Modern Architecture to Tropical Architecture. We also had a series of lectures from Bucky Fuller – I didn't understand much of it, but we did put his theories into practice, using very thin aluminium sheets to create a dome which we presented at the first Ghana Trade Fair and which housed university exhibits.

President Nkrumah brought in a lot of Eastern European architects, and some were very good. And he brought about the introduction of all these beautiful buildings. But I would echo Professor Ali Mazrui's line: Nkrumah was a very good African but a very poor Ghanaian. He brought politics into everything. I remember that he knew Victor Adegbite very well. Adegbite was the fifth Ghanian architect, who studied in America and was put in charge of the Ghana Housing Corporation. The first qualified architect in Ghana was Theodore Shealtiel Clerk, the second was D.K. Dawson, the third J.S.K. Frimpong. The fourth was Peter Turkson, who mostly practised planning and became the head of town planning at Tema. The fifth was Adegbite. And I was the sixth.

Senior Staff Clubhouse by
John Owusu Addo, KNUST, 1960s

A tool for Nehruvian national Modernism regeneration

(Previous spread) Habib Rahman showing
his first design for the Rabindra Bhavan
to Nehru and Achyut Kanvinde, 1961

The Sanskar Kendra or Museum of Knowledge designed by
Le Corbusier using his signature pilotis in Ahmedabad, 1954. The
building was the first home of the National Institute of Design. 158

Ram Rahman

Ram Rahman has photographed contemporary architecture across India for prominent architects. He has also curated exhibitions of Delhi's modern architecture and lectured on architecture and photography history. He is a founder of the activist artist collective SAHMAT. His photographs are in the collections of museums across the world.

Both my father Habib Rahman and Achyut Kanvinde had graduated with M.Arch degrees from MIT and Harvard respectively, and had returned to India by the second half of the 1940s, just as we were gaining independence from the British. By the late '40s Kanvinde had moved to New Delhi and begun designing for Government institutions, while Rahman moved to Delhi in 1952 to join the Central Public Works Department (CPWD). As fresh graduates without much building experience they did not have the organizational capabilities or the urban planning training required to manage and conceive a city-scale project like Chandigarh.

Le Corbusier was chosen as the leader of the team of architects and planners for Chandigarh after the tragic death of the Polish architect Matthew Nowicki in 1950. Nowicki had already prepared plans before his air crash, but no building had started. Le Corbusier, his cousin Jeanneret, Maxwell Fry and Jane Drew had considerable experience behind them, and the project was handed to them.

Rahman's contact with Jawaharlal Nehru was at the inauguration of Rahman's first built project – Gandhi Ghat, the first memorial in India to the assassinated Mahatma Gandhi, which was dedicated to the nation in 1949, a year after Gandhi's death. The structure, a Modernist expression combining Hindu, Muslim and Christian architectural elements stylized in plastered concrete, was on the bank of the River Ganges in Barrackpore, north of Calcutta. Nehru loved the structure and asked to meet the architect. Although Rahman had become close to Nehru's sister Vijaylakshmi Pandit in New York in the 1940s, this was his first meeting with Nehru and the beginning of a personal relationship.

At their meeting Nehru asked my father about his background and training, and said he must transfer to Delhi from the Bengal Public Works Department as architects like him (though few people used the word 'architect' in India at the time, 'engineer' being the more common term) were desperately needed for the building projects the government was about to initiate specially in the capital. It took a few years to finalize the transfer, which happened in 1952.

By then Rahman had designed over 80 projects for the government of West Bengal, including the large-scale New Secretariat and the Bengal Engineering College Buildings, and had gained considerable experience in publicly financed building. Having moved to New Delhi, his first project was helping to conceive the International Housing Exhibition in 1954. His own design for a two-room house was adapted on a mass scale into double storeyed blocks to house the expanding government employees streaming into Delhi as the government expanded post-independence. These were then built across India.

The first Indian chief architect of the Central Public Works Department in Delhi following independence was Bombay-trained G.B. Deolalikar. The prominent buildings he designed in Delhi were the Supreme Court of India (1959) and the National Museum (1961), which had aspects of the Lutyens 'Delhi Order' in their design. Both had red sandstone plinths and the Supreme Court building had a neo-Lutyens dome; Nehru disliked this feature and, in conversation with Rahman, referred to it as a colonial 'Solar Topee' (hat). Nehru also disliked the chattris (canopies) atop the office buildings built along the Rajpath central secretariat in the late 1950s, designed by the Bombay-trained CPWD architects Shridhar Joglekar and Jehangir Billimoria, but did not interfere with the chief architect's decision to go ahead with their construction as building had already started.

The issue of tradition and style for the newly independent nation was hotly debated by the young architects and artists from across India who attended the 1959 Lalit Kala National Symposium on Architecture in Delhi, convened by Achyut Kanvinde. In his inaugural address to the conference, Nehru was critical of adding elements of traditional architecture to modern buildings as a token of the past. He spoke of his admiration for Le Corbusier's design and mind, and described Chandigarh as opening the path to other experiments for the present and future of the changed socialist society which independence had brought into being.

This symposium led the call for architecture as an independent profession freed from the engineers who had dominated most public construction under the British. It was here that the first American-trained architects – Kanvinde, Rahman, Piloo Mody, Charles Correa – brought their different perspectives forward, in contrast to the older architects trained under British academies. The Bauhaus and American Modernist roots of both Rahman and Kanvinde found expression in the first office buildings they designed in Delhi; unlike the exposed concrete structures preferred by Le Corbusier in Chandigarh, their buildings were of plastered brick with sunshading louvres inspired by the Oscar Niemeyer structures they had seen in publications in Cambridge.

It was because of his Muslim family roots that Rahman, though a staunch secular non-believer, was asked in the late 1950s to design the tomb of the Muslim educationist and freedom fighter Maulana Azad, in front of the great seventeenth-century Mughal Jama Masjid mosque in old Delhi. He came up with a simple structure based on the arch of the mosque: a thin-shelled concrete cross-vault finished in a fine marble terrazzo. This Modernist tomb was opposed by conservative Muslim religious clergy, but Rahman's Muslim name (and the support of both Nehru and his Muslim officials) prevailed and the tomb was built. Nehru admired both this structure and Rahman's Gandhi Ghat for the way they evoked earlier Indian architecture but gave it a Modernist twist, both in form and material.

These experiments found their full expression in the Lalit Kala Akademi buildings and the Rabindra Bhavan cultural complex in New Delhi, finished in 1961. Rahman's first design for the latter, built in memory of the Bengali poet Rabindranath Tagore for his centenary, was an institutional Bauhaus-like box. Nehru hated it (he had a sharp temper) and berated Rahman, saying his design had nothing to do with the ethos of Tagore. Prodding Rahman to refer to the earlier monuments, Nehru got actively involved in the redesign of the final building, which used sloping walls of Delhi granite – inspired by the Sultanate architecture of medieval Delhi – as well as Mughal-inspired arch details, and made extensive use of modern geometric *jaalis*. This building became the stylistic breakthrough for Rahman and his later institutional buildings had more expressive flourishes than his pre-1961 works. The Rabindra Bhavan complex saw the resolution of his struggle to find an Indian idiom in a Modernist vocabulary: 'This building was the first where I broke out of the Oscar Niemeyer influence,' he said. 'This building belonged to India.' Unfortunately, it has suffered drastic alterations over the years, the most recent being a shoddy lift shaft being constructed outside the gallery block.

The early 1990s saw an opening up of the Indian economy, which had been under socialist protections from an open international trade in order to rebuild India's economic base (which had been destroyed under British colonial rule). As the consumerist economic boom progressed, in architecture, as in many other fields, international building trends became the norm. Characterless mirror-glass towers started sprouting across the country, and the visionary modern design that had inspired three generations of designers in socialist times could not stand up to the onslaught of the consumerist mall aspirations of the new generation. Government was no longer the biggest builder.

With the election of Narendra Modi as prime minister in 2014, there has been a fundamental shift in India's cultural landscape. Modi's mentor outfit is the Rashtriya Swayamsevak Sangh (RSS), a right-wing Hindu fundamentalist political organization now almost 100 years old which found inspiration in Mussolini's Blackshirts and admired Hitler's 'final solution' in Germany, and his government is following an increasingly virulent anti-Muslim and anti-Christian agenda. Modi has a hatred of Nehru and anything associated with what became known as the 'Nehru era'. In Delhi, this has manifested itself in actual large-scale demolitions of many of Delhi's modern landmarks.

Most shocking is the destruction, despite an international appeal to save it, of the Raj Rewal/Mahendra Raj Hall of Nations in 2017. At time of writing, four of Rahman's projects in Delhi have also been demolished, as has the entire Pragati Maidan – the trade fair venue and site of the Hall of Nations, which also had signature buildings from the 1970s and '80s by two generations of Modernists: Joseph Allen Stein, Ram Sharma, Kuldip Singh, Ranjit Sabikhi. The impending demolition of the National Museum will see it replaced by towering office blocks along the two sides of Lutyens's Central Vista promenade: a new fascist vision for the new Hindu nation.

The Chandigarh College of Architecture designed by
Aditya Prakash from a plan by Le Corbusier, with
administrative offices (left) and workshops (right)

Promotional material for the
film *Tere Ghar Ke Samne*, 1963

168

Chapter IV

In the 1963 Hindi romantic comedy *Tere Ghar Ke Samne* (In Front of Your House) an architect, played by Dev Anand, returns to Delhi from his architectural training in America to help build the new India. His father, who wears black-rimmed glasses and is, like his son, thoroughly westernized, has bought a plot of land at a government auction on which he wants his son to build him a house; the underbidder, who sports a traditional turban, ends up buying the less desirable back plot for a fraction more than he was outbid out of wounded pride and to score points. Unaware of the familial relationship, he also hires the architect to build his house, instructing him to make the one in front 'look like cow dung' beside his own. 'Why would you want to live next to cow dung?' the architect responds.

This client – for whom the American-trained architect designs a high-tech Modernist house with a curvaceous concrete façade and cantilevered balconies – has a daughter (played by Nutan) with whom the architect inevitably falls in love. When his own father stumbles across his futuristic design, he praises it and presumes it is for the house that he has commissioned. Thus, in this comedy of errors, the architect ends up designing identical Modernist dreamhouses for the two feuding neighbours. The young couple eventually marry in the courtyard created by these two bulbous homes, which verge on the Punjabi baroque, thereby peacefully uniting the warring families. It is an obvious metaphor for India putting aside differences to come together after Partition in a bright, harmonious, Modernist future.

Directed by Anand's younger brother Vijay Anand, the film contains a memorable scene in which the sophisticated central character, with his carefully brylcreemed hair and Italianate suit, pursues his future wife to Shimla and drives his Lambretta scooter through Chandigarh, the emblem of Modernist India. Le Corbusier's Capitol buildings are seen only in the distance and the greenery of 'The City Beautiful' is not quite as abundant as it is now, but the camera's focus is on the domestic-scale Tropical Modernism appropriate to the film's theme. *Tere Ghar Ke Samne* shows how Nehru's ideas of modernization and nation-building permeated popular culture and India's domestic fantasies. Everyone's lives could be transformed by Modernism's progressive ethos. The social message of the film is Nehruvian: not all that is new is bad, nor is all that is old good.

Nehru thought that the big houses being built after independence in Delhi – such as those that appear in the film, with their conspicuous display of black-market steel – were vulgar in the context of housing shortages. In Chandigarh, he had vetoed Le Corbusier's plans for the Governor's Palace, fronted by ramps and ponds, as 'undemocratic'.[1] The project had the geographic significance to Le Corbusier's scheme that the Viceroy's House had to Lutyens's New Delhi and would have completed Le Corbusier's vision for the Capitol Complex, but Nehru thought it distasteful to build such a palace at that time. The modest housing in Chandigarh – which did away, largely for economic reasons, with purdah screens and sweepers' passages, thereby challenging long-held social taboos – was more accessible and influential, and became the model for a new, progressive, cosmopolitan way of living. Eulie Chowdhury explained how it sought 'to interpret contemporary Indian life, which is a blend of traditional habits and Westernised ideas and which is changing rapidly in this fast-moving world'.[2]

Responding to an urgent need for housing, with many refugees from Partition still homeless and with so much new migration from villages to big cities, Nehru tasked the young architect Habib Rahman with organizing the International Exhibition on Low-Cost Housing in New Delhi in 1954. Rahman, like the hero of Tere Ghar Ke Samne, had trained in America under the influential German architect Walter Gropius. He represented a different Modernist tradition from Le Corbusier and his buildings preceded the latter's arrival in India. Rahman returned to India on the eve of independence and in 1948 designed a memorial near Calcutta to Mahatma Gandhi, recently assassinated by Hindu nationalist Nathuram Godse. Nehru's and Gandhi's belief in a secular India that respected all religions was enshrined in the constitution, and Nehru admired Rahman's design for its abstraction of forms from India's multiple faiths. He transferred Rahman to the Central Public Works Department in Delhi.

For the housing exhibition, architects from across India, including Rahman, built a village of 62 climate-responsive homes, all costing less than 5,000 rupees (then £400). Two of the houses were designed by Fry, Drew, Jeanneret and the Chandigarh team. In the model 'village' – the neighbourhood unit on which Gandhi had hoped to build a Ruskin-like arts and crafts utopian India – there also stood a replica of the hut in which the Mahatma had lived and worked. At the inauguration of the exhibition Nehru, Gandhi's former comrade, stated that 'a house is not merely a place to take shelter [and] the minimum accommodation that any family should have is two rooms, a kitchen, a lavatory and a small veranda. If possible, a little open space also.'[3] The exhibition, which was popular and well-attended (attracting 30,000 people), set a bar for living standards in post-independence India and created new expectations around privacy, hygiene and ventilation. It was an important demonstration and promotion of Modernism as a tool for progress and social welfare.

In 1957 Rahman was instrumental in founding the Delhi-based magazine Design, helping to recruit his former tutor Walter Gropius to serve on the editorial board and actively contributing to the journal from its first issue. An enthusiastic promoter of Nehruvian Modernism, the magazine reflected the exciting cosmopolitanism of the moment. It showcased a new emerging and aspirational middle class at home in Modernist interiors, surrounded by Modernist artworks and sprawling on Modernist furniture. The image of the urban sophisticate – more liberal and progressive than people from the surrounding villages and open to international influence and trends – was contagious. But post-colonial India, even though it wanted to catch up with the West with rapid industrialization and state-sponsored modernizing projects, also sought to define itself against the West. 'The modernism of the post-colonial Nehruvian state', writes Vikramaditya Prakash, was 'the self-empowering act of dissolving contradiction by simultaneously rejecting and appropriating the unsolicited gift of colonisation.'[4]

★

There was a battle in post-independence India between Modernists – who advocated an international, avant-garde approach to architecture that radically departed from the past – and revivalists, who wanted something more clearly Indian. As the architect and

Nehru at the opening of the Gandhi Ghat memorial, photographed by Habib Rahman, 1949

Habib Rahman in his studio, 1950s

educator B.M. Pradhan put it in 1959, one group 'advocated the use of traditional form, shape, in fact everything traditional with total regard to its suitability ... The second group, extremely revolutionary in spirit, probably because of the intense revolutionary atmosphere of the pre-independence era, wants to break away from all traditions.'[5] What united the two groups was that they had been educated either in the West, where they were exposed to western design principles, or through the western filters of such institutions as the Sir J.J. School of Architecture in Bombay, run by Claude Batley, a revivalist who dismissed Modernism as 'this new architecture'.[6] Both factions were therefore equally removed from traditional architecture, even if they were expected to be 'Indian' in their approach.

After a remark in Parliament by the Deputy Minister for Works, Housing and Supply, there were fears that government officials planned to introduce a national policy on architecture, similar to that seen in the Soviet Union or China, that would guide development in the new country. It would encourage the use of traditional motifs so that all new buildings could be given a clear Indian identity – whatever that was. Such a policy would unite and subordinate regional differences to a countrywide aesthetic. This disturbed Modernist architects, who were committed to an International Style that rejected both tradition and ornament, and they worried that their art would be put to the service of a sentimental nationalism and patriotic glorification. Despite Chandigarh, which sidestepped this question, and all his rhetoric about the 'temples of modern India', it wasn't absolutely clear where Nehru stood on the aesthetics of architecture.

This question of national style revived long-running debates from the early twentieth century, when Rabindranath Tagore and Ananda Coomaraswamy were keen to discourage the 'thoughtless imitation of unsuitable European habits and customs'.[7] But did a 'national style' refer to something made by Indian nationals, or to some spirit or essence that was essentially Indian? Nehru was something of a pragmatist, open to new ideas and keen to experiment, with an expansive, pluralist definition of Indianness. In *The Discovery of India* (1946) he described the country as 'an ancient palimpsest on which layer upon layer of

NEW - MAIN PIAZZA
indian institute of technology - kanpur

The Indian Institute of Technology
(IIT), Kanpur, designed by Achyut
Kanvinde, 1959–66

thought and reverie had been inscribed, and yet no succeeding layer had completely hidden or erased what had been written previously'.[8] When B.E. Doctor was designing the Ashoka Hotel in Delhi (1956), Nehru pressed the architect to add features such as latticed windows (*jaalis*), rooftop kiosks (*chhatris*) and other features that supposedly blended traditional Indian designs with the present-day comforts and amenities of the West. Modernists ridiculed this pastiche of Indian elements, but they also realized that the foreign architects they admired did not want to come to India to see pallid copies of their own architecture but a distinctive Tropical Modernism that reacted to the country's geography, climate, history and ideals.

In March 1959 Achyut Kanvinde – who had also trained in America under Walter Gropius – organized a conference and exhibition in Delhi to explore this question of national identity in building. Some 80 impassioned members of the architectural elite met to argue out their differences at the Lalit Kala Akademi in Jaipur House (now the National Gallery of Modern Art), established five years earlier to promote and propagate Indian art within and outside the country. The opening remarks of the Seminar on Architecture were addressed directly to Nehru:

> Today, there is construction of every type – public buildings for public purposes, or dwelling houses for the rich, the not-so-rich and the poor. There is an attempt, a concerted attempt, a social endeavour, to raise the standard of living of everybody. The State under the leadership of our Prime Minister is pledged to build a Welfare State in the country which will bring equal opportunities to all, which will give everybody the chance of blossoming into his or her fullest capacity. India today offers unrivalled opportunities to the artist as well.[9]

Nehru responded directly to the anxiety in the room, urging his audience not to be constrained by tradition and the beautiful but functionless baubles of the past, but to think in new terms: appreciating the social, economic and climatic context of India and

View of a walkway at the
Indian Institute of Technology
(IIT), Kanpur

responding to them with new materials suitable to the industrial age. 'Traditions are good, but no tradition which imprisons your mind is worth accepting,' he said reassuringly. 'You should accept tradition but not coercion.'[10] He talked about his 'great experiment' at Chandigarh, which was intended to challenge the past: 'Many people argue about it, some like it, some dislike it.' He said:

> It is totally immaterial, whether you like it or not; it is the biggest job of its kind in India. That is why I welcome it. It is the biggest because it hits you on the head, because it makes you think. You may squirm at the impact but it makes you think and imbibe new ideas and, the one thing that India requires in so many fields is to be hit on the head so that you may think.[11]

In his own talk Kanvinde noted that the post-independence building boom offered 'a great opportunity and posed a challenge to Indian architects to create and evolve an architecture which should establish the mark of our time'.[12] He urged his peers to find a new Indian architecture that resisted blindly copying European Modernism and avoided the decorative pastiche favoured by revivalists, but which did not refuse to turn to the past for inspiration. Just back from Harvard, Kanvinde's early work – such as the Ahmedabad Textile Industry's Research Association (ATIRA) building, inaugurated by Nehru in 1954 – looks like Gropius's Bauhaus buildings transported to the Tropics. In the late 1950s, Kanvinde began to move away from the strict functionalism of the Bauhaus style and sought a more human scale. Buildings such as the Indian Institute of Technology (IIT) campus in Kanpur (1959–66) were miniature cities, adopting principles of climate control influenced by vernacular architecture.

New Delhi, where the Seminar on Architecture met, was itself in flux and a new masterplan had been commissioned to address the problems of its rapid growth, which included epidemics of jaundice and cholera. In 1956 the Delhi Development Authority was founded and Gordon Cullen, a British attendee of the conference, was working on a radical plan for New Delhi's imperial centre that was represented in the accompanying exhibition.

Reflecting Nehru's dislike for the 'ghost-like' buildings of the past, it broke the intimidatingly colonial 'Lutyens axis' with the bold addition of Modernist towers and plazas. These surrounded and disrupted the massive imperial rotunda of Parliament House, where Nehru had given his 1947 'Tryst with Destiny' speech, and were intended to signal a new democratic direction. Though this vision ultimately went unrealized, many other attendees of the seminar built some of the Modernist landmarks that would come to define New Delhi.

Nehru granted these architects their creative freedom and no national policy emerged, but he continued to have a keen interest in architecture. In 1959 Habib Rahman was designing the Rabindra Bhavan, a new arts complex for Lalit Kala Akademi and one of a series of structures intended to celebrate the centenary of Rabindranath Tagore, the poet, artist and social reformer who had invited the Bauhaus to exhibit in Calcutta in 1922 alongside contemporary artists from the Bengali avant-garde such as Sunayan Devi, Nandalal Bose, Jamini Roy, and Gaganendranath and Abanindranath Tagore.

Apparently, Nehru disliked Rahman's original Bauhaus-like design (rejecting it as 'nonsense', according to Rahman's son, the photographer and historian Ram Rahman).[13] He considered it too European and, in light of the mood of the Seminar, encouraged Rahman to design something instead that displayed a modern Indian spirit – which the architect did, very much under Nehru's direction. There are photographs of Nehru sneering at a model of the original design, and of him looking over the architect's shoulder at drawings of new plans.

Ultimately, when completed in 1961, Rahman's building was dominated by sweeping concrete sunshades, and employed a Modernist architectural language combined with abstracted Indian references including Mughal arches, latticed screens (jaalis) and the use of Delhi quartzite stone. It occupied a centre ground that recalled the philosopher Isaiah Berlin's description of Rabindranath Tagore: 'He never showed his wisdom more clearly than in choosing the difficult middle path, drifting neither to the Scylla of radical modernism, nor to the Charybdis of proud and gloomy traditionalism.'[14]

Reimagining of India's
parliament building
in New Delhi by Gordon
Cullen, 1961

Habib Rahman explaining plans of the
Rabindra Bhavan to Nehru, 7 May 1961; and
(opposite) the architect's own photographs
of the arts complex, New Delhi, 1961

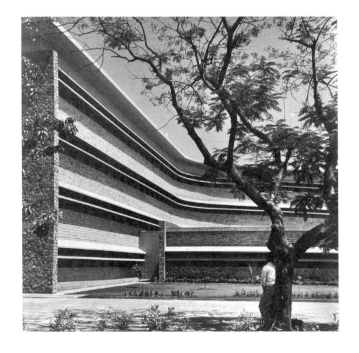

The Sarabhai House designed by
Le Corbusier in Ahmedabad, 1951–6

★

In the early 1960s a new generation of architecture schools began to emerge in India, seeking to foster a distinctive Indian Modernism that didn't just imitate the West but was more attuned to the country's traditions. But the post-colonial dilemma remained, as Vikramaditya Prakash puts it: 'how to define an authentic "non-west", beyond the stranglehold of [western] "orientalism"'.[15] In 1961, following the recommendations of American designers Ray and Charles Eames, the National Institute of Design (NID) was established in Ahmedabad. Architect Balkrishna Doshi was involved in the founding of NID, which taught architecture until 1969; alongside this, he began his own architecture school, the Centre of Environmental Planning and Technology (CEPT). The Chandigarh College of Architecture was also founded in 1961. At all three institutions the search for an Indian Modernist identity became an intellectual project and tool for national regeneration.

A key figure in this story of architectural education in India was Gira Sarabhai, an intensely private architect whose contribution to Indian Modernism has been insufficiently recognized. She was the youngest of the eight children of the textile magnate Amabalal Sarabhai, a prominent supporter of India's independence struggle and of Mahatma Gandhi, whose Sabarmati Ashram was located in Ahmedabad – indeed, several members of the Sarabhai family spent time in prison because of their support of Gandhi. However, as a modernizer and the first person in the city to own an automobile, Amabalal Sarabhai did not share Gandhi's fetishization of the spinning wheel (*charkha*) and village life. All but one of his children were home-schooled in the Montessori method before being sent to study in the West. (Only Gira's sister Mridula refused, faithfully sticking to Gandhi's boycott of foreign goods and institutions.)

Gira Sarabhai trained as an architect under Frank Lloyd Wright at his Taliesin West studio in Arizona, where she worked on the spiral shell design for New York's Solomon R. Guggenheim Museum. In 1946 she commissioned Wright to design an administrative office and store for the family firm in Ahmedabad, but it never got off the drawing board. Like her siblings, Sarabhai returned to India to contribute to Nehru's post-independence modernization project – Nehru was a family friend – and cemented the family's reputation for patronage as the 'Medicis of Ahmedabad'. In 1949 she designed the Calico Museum of Textiles, in the Calico Mills compound, the first Modernist building in Ahmedabad (the city was a centre of textile production, known in the nineteenth century as the 'Manchester of India'). She also curated the new museum's unrivalled collection of Indian contemporary and historic fabrics, intended as a research collection that would contribute to the improvement of Indian design.

Having fallen out with Wright, Gira switched allegiance to Le Corbusier, who was then in India building Chandigarh. (Gira's nephew Suhrid Sarabhai owns a letter his formidable aunt sent Le Corbusier, thanking him for sending a book about himself and confessing bluntly that she won't read it as she does not understand French.) In 1951 she invited Le Corbusier to Gujarat, hoping that he might be persuaded to build a house for her recently widowed sister-in-law Manorama and her two children. He ended up building two luxury villas in Ahmedabad as well as the Sanskar Kendra museum and the Mill Owner's Association Building, a porous cube whose façade is covered in a sun breaker, or brise soleil, that also serves as planters for hanging gardens. Le Corbusier intended this 'little palace' – which builds on the theories developed in his Tower of Shadows at Chandigarh – as a prototype for 'modern architecture adjusted to the climate of India'.[16] Balkrishna Doshi, who worked in Le Corbusier's Paris studio from 1951 to '54 (the first eight months unpaid) returned to India as site architect for these projects, before setting up his own practice in Ahmedabad, taking Corbusier's lofty grammar and infusing it with a more democratic Indian spirit.

Today, the Villa Sarabhai is part of the family estate, known as 'the Retreat'. The villa is open plan, with a series of tiled barrel vaults that look on to a verdant garden, closed to the elements only with bamboo blinds. A photograph shows Suhrid Sarabhai with Le Corbusier and Doshi discussing the 13.7m (45-foot) slide that comes down from the roof, which Sarabhai claims was his idea, and drops into a swimming pool that Corbusier had argued should be bigger. The architect also lost the battle against having fans, which were later painted by Robert Rauschenberg and claimed as artistic mobiles.

The Retreat was the focus of the Sarabhai family's international patronage: as well as Le Corbusier, Gira Sarabhai invited Alexander Calder, Isamu Noguchi, John Cage, Henri Cartier-Bresson, Richard Neutra and Charles and Ray Eames to stay and for residencies in a garden studio. In 1958 Nehru commissioned the Eameses to write their *India Report*, which recommended a school of design on the Bauhaus model with students 'learning by doing'. The NID, for which the projected school was a blueprint, opened in 1961 as an important part of Nehru's industrialization strategy. Its first home, funded by the Sarabhais, was in a studio at Calico Mills before it moved to Le Corbusier's empty museum building, designed a decade earlier. In 1966 Gira and her brother Gautam, a Cambridge-educated mathematician, completed a new campus for the NID on the banks of the Sabarmati river, which they designed with courtyard teaching spaces and a roof of elegant brick dome vaults.

One of the NID's first projects was the creation of the Indian Institute of Management (IIM), established by Gira's eldest brother, the physicist and astronomer Vikram Sarabhai, who initiated India's space programme (for which Shivdatt Sharma became chief architect). Working with NID students and faculty, Doshi served as project architect under Louis Kahn, then completing the National Parliament building in East Pakistan (now Bangladesh). Kahn created a red-brick behemoth, punctuated by huge round, semi-circular and square windows that act as geometric filters for sunlight and ventilation. He was influenced by the mysterious and surprisingly minimal eighteenth-century Jantar Mantar observatory in Delhi, and his use of local materials and monumental and geometric making of space would exert considerable influence on Doshi and other Indian architects. The stark simplicity of Charles Correa's Gandhi Memorial Museum at the Sabarmati Ashram, for example, with its modular clusters of buildings with pyramidal roofs that marry tradition and modernity and symbolize Gandhi's moral restraint and village utopia, reflects Kahn's influence.

In 1962 Doshi also established and designed a separate School of Architecture in Ahmedabad, which became the Centre

Balkrishna Doshi teaching at CEPT, the architecture school he founded and designed, 1966

Doshi in Le Corbusier's Paris office, early 1950s

of Environmental Planning and Technology (CEPT). The school's non-hierarchical curriculum was reflected in Doshi's campus building, which had fluid, multi-use spaces including an open undercroft for teaching that linked raised lawns on one side with a sunken courtyard on the other, and breezy, bright interconnected studios above. It followed the philosophy of Tagore's Shantiniketan school (which became Visva Bharati University in 1921), whose curriculum united art and science and where classes were held outdoors in an effort to integrate the school with the community. CEPT was to follow a similar model of social and cultural renewal for a post-independence India in which local and foreign ideas would mix and ferment and both could be confidently claimed as Indian.

NID students embarked on fieldwork to document and upgrade traditional Indian crafts, and helped build Gira and Gautam Sarabhai's Buckminster Fuller-inspired Calico Dome (1963), the first space frame structure in India, which was raised over the foundations for Frank Lloyd Wright's abandoned building. Students from Doshi's architecture school travelled India to measure and record the country's stepwells, mosques and temples and to study rural villages and towns. Rather than appropriating this architecture as a device to express national identity, they rediscovered and updated traditional design solutions to climate and living. While the heavy parasol roof of Doshi's Institute of Indology reflects Le Corbusier's lingering influence, he came to think of Le Corbusier's buildings as 'foreign and out of milieu' (which reflected the 1960s critiques of Le Corbusier by Team X, Jane Jacobs and Norma Evenson).[17] Reacting to Chandigarh, which discouraged mixed-income neighbourhoods and informal street markets, Doshi sought to combine modern and indigenous principles in new architectural expressions.

CEPT was a building designed to be added to as the student body increased, with concrete lintels jutting from the flanks of the structure as invitations to new designs. Complexes such as Doshi's Life Insurance Corporation housing development in Ahmedabad similarly sought to create an architectural frame that could be added to by the inhabitants using a kit of elements, thereby reintroducing the vitality of informal architecture and

India's public spaces to a sterile Modernism. Houses were stacked in three ownership tiers with the most expensive at the bottom and the cheapest at the top, creating a mixed-income neighbourhood that has been continuously adapted by its long-term owners with additions and extensions, no two alike.

In 1967 Aditya Prakash became principal of the Chandigarh College of Architecture (CCA), the institution that had been suggested by the Modern Architecture Club Prakash had founded to unite the Indian architects working on the Chandigarh project. Inaugurated in 1961, the college occupied a building that Prakash had adapted from an earlier design by Le Corbusier when working on the Chandigarh team. He had scaled down Le Corbusier's Modulor man to fit Indian brick sizes, and his architecture school is therefore a slightly diminutive version of the art school Le Corbusier built in a nearby sector, with its factory-like roofs flooding the studios below with warm light. It was located next to the Punjab Engineering College designed by J.K. Chowdhury, enabling a constant dialogue between the two disciplines.

At CCA Prakash began urban research that led him to question Le Corbusier's city plan, with its lifeless Capitol screened off from the rest of the city by bunker-like mounds and its eccentric rules ('For the Establishment of an Immediate Statute of the Land') banning cows and informal markets. The Capitol was a symbol of progress and democracy that did little to address real human needs: 'It's a place for gods to play; it's not for humans,' Prakash said.[18] The challenge for Indian architects was, he thought, to extricate themselves from the 'make-believe world' of foreign influence and to think independently. 'Everything I have learnt that has really been of value, I have learnt from Le Corbusier – even if it has been by going against him,' Prakash said. 'By arguing with Le Corbusier, in my own mind, I have become who I am.'[19]

His curriculum was based on 'live' projects led by the faculty and on the critical interrogation of the Chandigarh experiment. Following research projects into vibrant bazaars in the cities surrounding Chandigarh, Prakash created models of the mobile street furniture used by informal street vendors in Chandigarh and used them to question Chandigarh's founding principles. In the early 1970s he developed alternative plans for a 'Linear City',

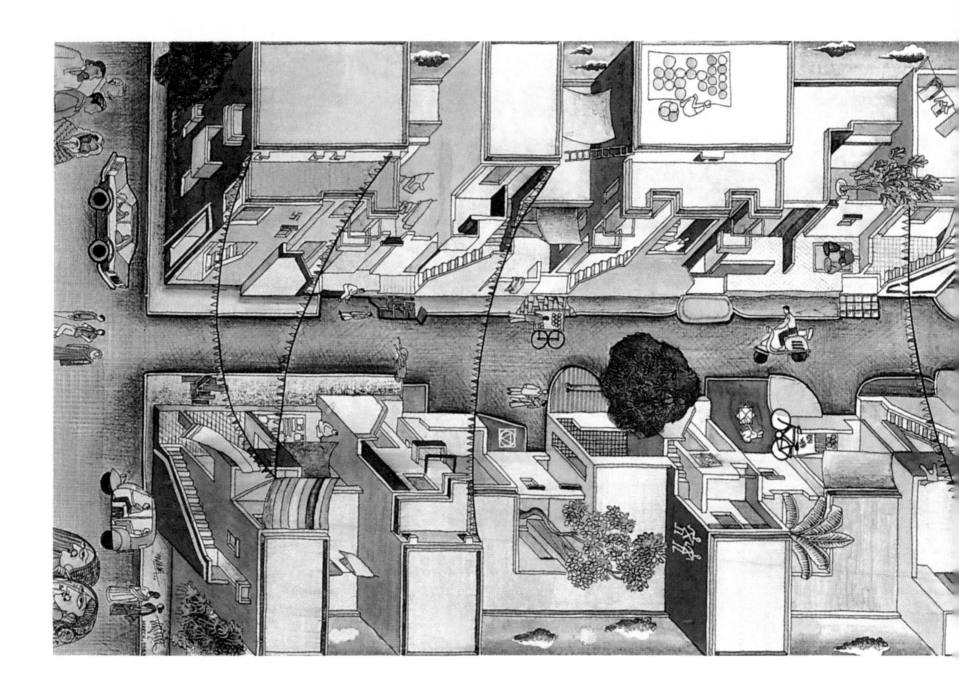

Balkrishna Doshi's painting of
Aranya Housing, *c.*1989

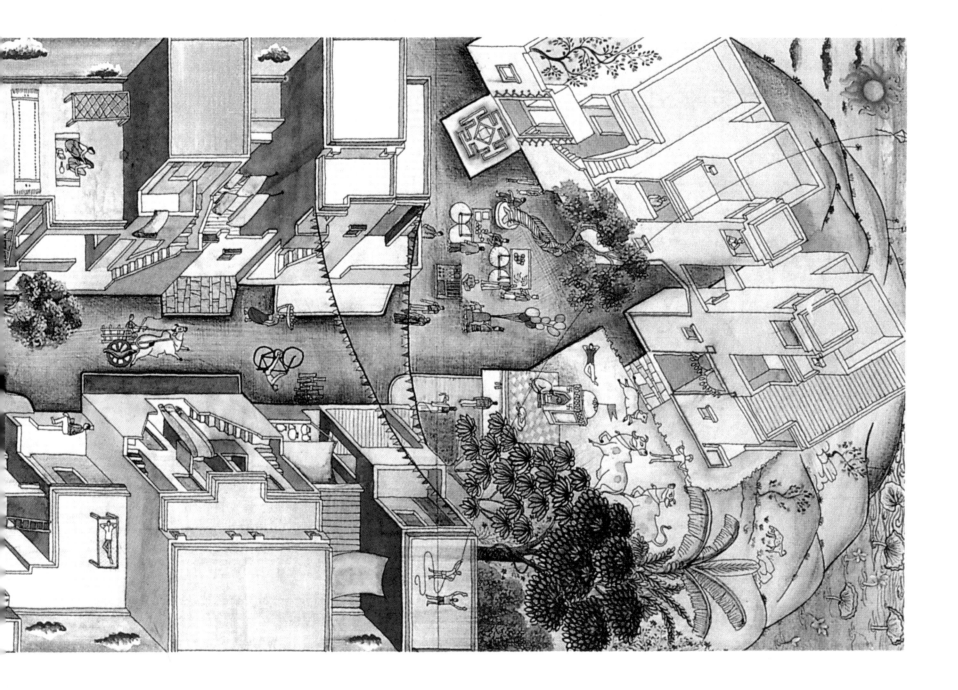

influenced by Buckminster Fuller's utopian thinking, that would reimagine Chandigarh. Axonometric views and perspective drawings drawn by Prakash show it as only a few sectors deep, but extending in a straight line across India. The urban and rural were therefore linked, with fields and irrigation canals within easy reach of every sector. Elevated highways allowed space beneath for a self-sustaining pedestrian haven with shops, markets and green spaces that, as with Doshi's designs, embraced India's lively street and village culture with its rickshaws, rehris (food carts) and cows.

★

'In 1965, soon after becoming chief architect [of Chandigarh],' recalled M.N. Sharma, 'I used my modest savings, hired a photographer, and took leave of two months to visit villages in India, including the hilly regions and plains of Punjab and Haryana.'[20] Sharma had a sense that the vernacular architecture of the region – the sculptural forms and handmade mud houses that Le Corbusier had admired and then replaced – were in decline. 'The geometric, masculine shapes of the Punjab villages of my childhood were worth documenting,' Sharma said.[21] Though he was a defender of the Le Corbusian faith to the last, his new interest in local architecture reflected a fresh regionalism that was increasingly critical of Le Corbusier's European imposition and celebrated the ways in which his architecture had been appropriated and adapted to make Chandigarh a truly Indian city.

In 1973 a highways engineer called Nek Chand came on his worn-out old bike to see Sharma and ask the architect if he could show him the secret garden he had been working on since 1958. 'I was amazed by what I saw,' Sharma said of his first visit to Chand's magical rock garden.[22] Chand had moved to India during Partition in 1947, finding work as a road inspector in Chandigarh. Perhaps out of nostalgia for his own, lost village, he began collecting discarded material from the construction of the new city, recycling it into a 'Secret Kingdom' that included over 2,000 sculptures and 20,000 river stones artfully arranged in a 12-acre complex of courtyards and waterfalls in a forest just a few hundred yards east of the Capitol Complex. Chand described his labyrinthine fantasy as a 'vast ruin, sighing to the winds' and a 'tale

Postcard from Pierre Jeanneret to Aditya Prakash recalling their inspirational trip to a Chandigarh scrapheap, 1961

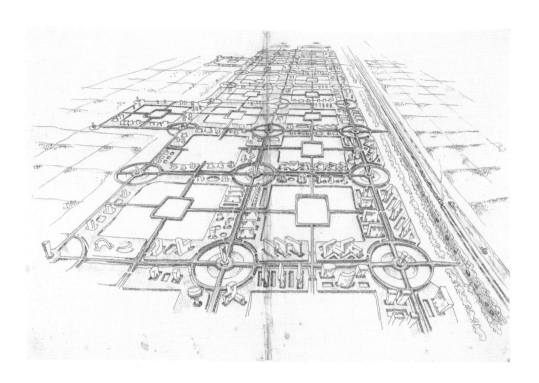

Sketch perspective of Linear
City, Chandigarh by Aditya
Prakash, *c.*1975

Nek Chand's Rock Garden,
Chandigarh, begun in 1958

of lost pomp and glory': 'Once upon a time a king and queen loved and lived here, dined and danced, fought and triumphed … and then their kingdom collapsed at the zenith of their power.'[23]

'It was an uncanny arrangement of space, using naturally sculpted stone and waste material,' Sharma recalled. 'I recognised at once Nek Chand's genius and also recognised that he had created his "Dream World" illegally … I was in deep conflict for a short while, but looking at this wonderful and unique artwork, I did not have the heart to go strictly by the rules.'[24] It was amazing to everybody that Chand had kept his work secret from the Chandigarh planning authorities for 15 years, and how much he had achieved in that period, working on his scheme in every moment of his free time. Sharma, who was also an amateur sculptor, compared Chand to Antoni Gaudi and Henry Moore and resolved to help him. In 1976, following an outpouring of public support, Chand was released from his highways duties and made superintendent of his garden, with 50 labourers allocated to help him complete his endeavour. Today it is one of Chandigarh's main tourist attractions.

In the 1961 issue of *Marg* on Chandigarh, Pierre Jeanneret wrote about finding beauty in found objects. Aditya Prakash had been inspired by the steel offcuts he found on a scrap-heap he visited with Jeanneret, using their accidental patterns in the shuttering on the façade of his Tagore Theatre. Like Chand, Jeanneret was a great collector of stones collected from the Shivalik Hills and Ghaggar riverbed, using them as decoration and to make handsome rubble masonry walls. Jeanneret's housekeeper, cook and driver, known as Bansai Lai, was a good friend of Chand's and some of Lai's sketches of snakes, jaguars and lizards were woven into carpets of Jeanneret's design – indeed, Chand may have been inspired in his enterprise by his visits to Pierre Jeanneret's house. Le Corbusier also shared Jeanneret's appreciation for folk art: he appropriated graffiti he saw a donkey driver sketch into wet concrete, copying it and reusing it in a commemorative block sited along the promenade of Sukhna Lake.

However, Chand's labyrinthine rock garden, built in the shadow of Le Corbusier's signature buildings, was a kind of outsider artist's critique of the architect's strict Modernist grid.

'The city and my garden are as different as the sky and the earth,' Chand said. When Fry revisited Chandigarh, touring the site with Sharma many years after he worked there, he observed how its commercial areas lacked 'the intimacy, even the untidiness, of the typical Indian bazaar'. Instead there were 'treeless blocks of unidentifiable blankness that verged on the vacantly forbidding':

I imagined that [Le Corbusier] peopled his buildings, where indeed they gave the appearance of being peopled, by figments of his own creation, unendowed with normal human attributes; and that as he grew older and more withdrawn, these counted for less than the elemental forms reaching forward to ultimate ruination.[25]

Chand's secret garden, already a ruin in the shadow of the Capitol Complex, was hidden behind a wall of shuttering that Chand made by filling tar drums with concrete; a door made of battered blue drums swings open on a hinged frame. Inside are walkways with large, neatly spaced river stones, chosen because Chand might have seen forms in their jagged shapes, each one carried back on his bicycle. Walls made of ceramic electrical three-point sockets resemble an ossuary of skulls, and low doors force visitors to bow down in respect before Chand's artwork. Rammed earth was made in split barrels tied together with coir ropes, then stacked to form columns finished in mud plaster. There are 20m (66ft) waterfalls which roar from Mughal-like structures crowned with *chhatris*, and quiet amphitheatres and cavernous passages whose high walls, made of concrete cast in jute sacks, are themselves covered in the concrete tendrils of imaginary banyan trees.

Chand transformed coal slag, lime-kiln waste, pebbles, crockery, smashed neon tubes and discarded glass bangles into a Noah's Ark of monkeys, leopards, elephants, buffalo, long-necked birds and cats with arched backs and anthropoid faces, watched over by a terracotta army of guards, musicians and other dancing human forms. Some of these colourful figures carry baskets on

Nehru with his deputy prime minister,
Vallabhai Patel, and the late Gandhi
watching from the clouds, *c.*1948

their heads like the anonymous workforce that built Chandigarh, Nehru's largest Modernist project, an urban essay in climate control (the Prime Minister was sometimes depicted in popular culture driving the seven-horse chariot of Surya, the solar deity in Hinduism). The hut at the centre of the garden, which used to be Chand's site office, has beaten-out tar drums for a roof, and now contains a waxwork of the artist, frozen in work. His derelict kingdom, a lost and found city, writes Iain Jackson, was 'an Indian piece built outside of direct European influence but on the spoils of modernity'.[26]

Sangath, the studio and architectural office Balkrishna Doshi
designed for himself in Ahmedabad, 1981, featuring a series of
sunken vaults covered in china mosaic and a grass amphitheatre

Raj Rewal

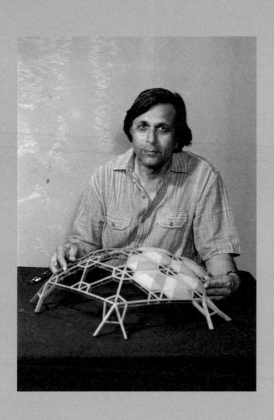

Raj Rewal is recognized internationally for buildings that respond sensitively to the complex demands of rapid urbanization, climate and culture. His works have been exhibited widely and are a part of the permanent collections of the Pompidou, MOMA, M+, and V&A. He is the recipient of many honours, including the Gold Medal given by the Indian Institute of Architects, the Robert Mathew Award by the Commonwealth Association of Architects and Chevalier de l'Ordre National de la Légion d'Honneur by the French Government.

Nehru was Modernism personified. His outlook was very modern, very rationalistic; he called for Indians to have a scientific temperament. On his visit to the Bhakra Nangal Dam he declared it a 'temple of new India', and he created the Indian Institutes of Technology – all these networks of engineering and technology, places of higher education. When people complained about Le Corbusier or Chandigarh, Nehru said that even he did not understand what was going on there, but that we should allow it to go on. He was a very liberal person, truly an intellectual.

Modernism didn't start with the Bauhaus. It started with Fatehpur Sikri, near Agra, because it is a very pure structure. Even Le Corbusier himself did drawings of the observatory at Jantar Mantar, and quotes it in the sweeping roof of the Assembly at Chandigarh. In 1985 I was the curator of the Festival of India exhibition, *Architecture en Inde* at the Ecole Nationale Supérieure des Beaux-Arts, Paris, which looked anew at our architectural heritage; for this, 60 architects and students meticulously measured then made drawings and models of sites I thought were in some way modern, all of which were secular and had something to do with function: I thought the stepwells of Ahmedabad, for example, were very modern.

The question Modernism asked was: how do you design in a hot climate? And the answer was already to be found in Fatehpur Sikri, Jaisalmer, Datia and Orchha, as well as the old towns of Rajasthan. There was not even a fan when these structures were built, yet they have very good ventilation: you walk through them and you don't feel so hot. The morphology or typology of space in these places made a lot of sense applied to modern architecture. That was the lesson I took for the athlete's village I built for the 1982 Asian Games in New Delhi. Like much of my work, it can be described as modern architecture with Indian roots, with an Indian ethos. I'm sure that it was also from indigenous architecture that Maxwell Fry and Jane Drew learned the traditional values which could be fused with the modern.

Nehru's daughter Indira Gandhi should also be considered a Modernist. I won the competition to do the Hall of Nations and Hall of Industries site at Pragati Maidan in Delhi when she was prime minister. This was for the Asia 72 global fair and I was only 36 years old at the time. My proposal was for a building that had a span of 256 feet. Nothing like that had ever been built before in concrete at this scale, so there were a few raised eyebrows.

Whereas Le Corbusier did buildings in concrete then put a sunbreaker on the façade, I designed a building that was itself a sunbreaker, a three-dimensional *jaali*. The depth of the structure, at 16 feet, became a sunbreaker, and for many years it did not have glass but was open, so it had the air circulating through it. It did not need air conditioning. Climatically it may be the most important building ever built.

We only had two years to complete it. India at that time could not make steel tubes, but my thesis at the Brixton School of Building in London had been on hyperbolic paraboloids and I knew that Pier Luigi Nervi had built his hall for the Turin Exhibition in 1949 with concrete trusses. I went to visit that building before we broke ground. I knew the structural engineer Mahendra Raj, who had worked with Corbusier in Chandigarh, and he took up the challenge.

We had thought we might use prefabricated parts, but no contractor would quote for that, so it was all done with *in situ* concrete. You make a wooden box, put steel rods in it, and pour in the concrete. That's it. The project was completed in just over a year and a half, with about 300–400 families living on site. Children were born there. It was almost a medieval thing: Chandigarh was also built like this. Women would carry the concrete in buckets on their heads and it was poured into the wooden shuttering, made by 50 or so carpenters. After the fourth or fifth floor, because of the space frame, it became very stable, and the work easier.

Six months before we were due to finish, they asked me to do the Nehru Pavilion, near the Hall of Nations in Pragati Maidan, as well. I was spending 18 hours a day on site and I didn't think I could handle it. I suggested they give it to Charles Correa or Balkrishna Doshi, but they weren't in Delhi, so I was persuaded to take it on. I reread Nehru's book *The Discovery of India* (1946), in which Nehru wrote about the difficulties uniting people with diverse languages, religions and cultural values.

The museum-pavilion would enshrine and celebrate Nehru's ideas, values, and ideals – inclusive growth, democracy, and the upliftment of all sections of society. Nehru was not only a great leader of India but of Asia and the developing world as a whole. He was a visionary with modern concerns. Nehru represented the spirit of new India on the one hand, as well as the austere values of Mahatma Gandhi. He imbibed the ideals of democracy and secular values along with nation-building strategies.

Because Nehru was agnostic, if not atheist – almost a Buddhist – I started thinking of making a building that was like a green stupa. I had seen something a bit like that in Nepal. The pavilion was a modern building but, as can be seen from the plan, it again has its roots in the Jantar Mantar. The building was totally non-monumental because I thought Nehru (who was considered Chacha Nehru – 'Uncle Nehru') would be the kind of person who would have hated a monument. It was built into a mound and, besides the green stupa, my idea was that children would run up and down the mound, which they did – it was amazing to see.

The Design Institute of Ahmedabad had all the material from the touring exhibition they'd designed about Nehru's life with Charles and Ray Eames, and they worked with me to put it on the ground floor. The exhibition covered Nehru's childhood, his education in England, his marriage, and projects for which he should be remembered such as the Bhakra Nangal Dam, Chandigarh and the Department of Atomic

Energy. All this was displayed on a freestanding bamboo frame wrapped in Indian fabric, so it had a very Indian look, like Rajasthan clothes.

On the first floor we showed films from the archive: Nehru's speeches, his All-India Radio Broadcasts. It was a great pleasure to hear Nehru talking – he was a very passionate man. In one of the museum's exhibition panels, Eames quotes Nehru on India: 'What have I discovered? She is a myth and an idea, a dream and a vision and yet very real and present and pervasive. There are terrifying glimpses of dark corridors which seem to lead back to the primaeval night, but also there is the fullness and warmth of the day about her.'

But the land on which the Hall of Nations and Industries Complex and Nehru Pavilion were built is very valuable – and, in addition, the Modi government wants to demolish anything to do with Nehruvian values. A proposal to redevelop Pragati Maidan was unveiled in 2015. There was outrage across Asia and the world through ARCASIA (Architects Regional Council Asia) and the Union of International Architects, who pleaded with Prime Minister Narendra Modi to spare these buildings, as they form an integral part of India's iconic architecture.

The Indian Institute of Architects went to the courts to fight it, while INTACH (Indian National Trust for Art and Cultural Heritage), a semi-government organization, also took legal action to try to preserve the Hall of Nations. But they all lost, and finally I had to hire a lawyer myself – the wife of an architect who was very passionate about it. The judge told her that he would consider the case in four days' time. But if it had gone to the Supreme Court, things would have been delayed a year, and the government didn't want that. The very next morning they went in with the bulldozers and demolished it.

The Indian Institute of Management by Louis Kahn,
Ahmedabad, 1974. The campus, with its porous, geometric
façades is currently at risk of demolition.

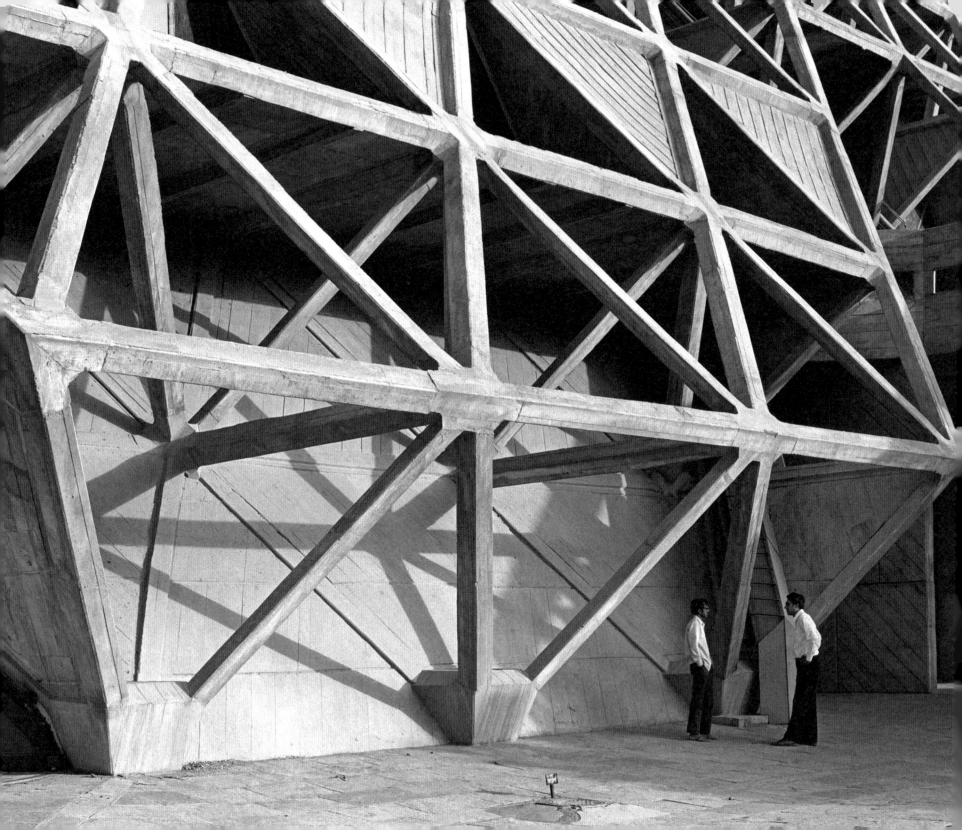

A Future for Tropical Modernism

(Previous spread) The Hall of Nations
by Raj Rewal, New Delhi, 1972

The International Trade Fair Center in Labadi, Accra
was completed in 1967 by the Ghana National Construction
Corporation (GNCC), led by Victor Adegbite

Fallen statue of Kwame Nkrumah
following the 1966 coup

Epilogue

In 1964, after a rigged referendum, Nkrumah appointed himself president of Ghana for life. He outlawed all political parties except the CPP, making the country a one-party state, claiming that this was the only way of combating Africa's great challenges of 'poverty, hunger, illiteracy, disease, ignorance, squalor, and low productivity'.[1] Several attempts had been made on his life, and he became increasingly paranoid: soon, speaking disrespectfully about the president became a criminal offence punishable by imprisonment. He passed laws that enabled him to incarcerate his political opponents, and had three of his former ministers executed. Students at his Winneba Ideological Institute (where Robert Mugabe was a pupil) and members of the Youth Pioneers group he initiated were drilled in Nkrumaism, taught slogans such as 'Nkrumah is our Messiah' and 'Nkrumah does no wrong'.[2]

However, following the collapse in the price of cocoa, which made up two-thirds of the country's exports, and after the expense of his industrial strategy, the country was almost bankrupt, with a balance of payments crisis and crippling level of inflation. Nkrumah was accused of squandering precious state resources on boondoggles such as the presidential lodge that Victor Adegbite had designed for him near Aburi, and Job 600, built for the 1965 Organisation of African Unity conference. Mired in corruption scandals, Nkrumah was politically vulnerable, and in 1966 he was overthrown in a military coup supported by the CIA, who were increasingly concerned by his pro-communist leanings. The many statues of Nkrumah, part of the cult of personality he sought to build around himself, were torn down and dismembered by a jubilant crowd.

The first radio broadcast of the military junta that toppled him announced to the nation: 'We lived our lives perpetually afraid of prison, poverty, and unaware of our future. Glorious dreams were continuously unfolded before our eyes. And this beloved country of ours was plunged into a dark night of misery and suffering. Nkrumah and his henchmen became rich, confident, and lorded it over us with all the ruthless instruments at their disposal – security forces, prisons and torture.'[3] Nkrumah subsequently lived in exile in Guinea, the country to which Ghana had been so financially generous, where he had the honorary title of

Co-President. His children, who moved to Cairo with their Egyptian mother, never saw him again.

Two months after Nkrumah's deposition, John Lloyd returned to London to head up the Architectural Association, and for many years Kwame Nkrumah University of Science and Technology was forced to drop Nkrumah's name. Large construction projects in Ghana dried up and architects who had been enticed back to the country by Nkrumah, such as Victor Adegbite and Max Bond, returned to America, where they had illustrious careers. John Owusu Addo moved for a time to Nigeria to take advantage of the post-war oil boom there.

At around that time, in parallel with Ghana's economy, Tropical Modernism began a slow decline, its principles of climate control made redundant above all by the ubiquity of the air-conditioning unit. 'Air-conditioning produces an anonymous architecture,' lamented Jane Drew in notes towards a memoir. 'A useless international style not quite useless except that it is very expensive and seems to be immoral in a world where so many people are in need, and now we know what we are doing to the ozone layer we have much to consider' (Fry retired in 1973 and Drew in 1979).[4] The open, perforated façades of Tropical Modernism that they had pioneered and which facilitated cross-ventilation were entombed in glass.

The Tropics were a laboratory for British architects and, following their colonial-era experiments with climate, their ideas might be seen as having returned to the metropolis to help define a more sustainable world. Indeed, in the 1970s and '80s, Tropical Modernism inspired a new sustainable ethos and aesthetic. Architects such as Richard Rogers, Norman Foster and Nicholas Grimshaw were inspired by Tropical Modernism's fusion of the International Style with 'scientific' climate control. Visually, early hi-tech buildings, with their Meccano-like, sectional engineering, owed more to Jean Prouvé, who chaired the 1971 committee that selected Rogers and Renzo Piano's design for the Pompidou Centre, a pop art homage to the master. The golden louvres on Foster's Bloomberg building in London are a last vestige of this, as hi-tech architecture ballooned in scale and, in a world of globalized commerce, strayed from its eco-sustainable roots.

★

Jawaharlal Nehru died in 1964, having served as prime minister of India for 16 years, but Tropical Modernism lived on in the country in increasingly large-scale and expressive structures until architecture took a postmodern turn in the early 1980s. In 1972, the year of Nkrumah's death, architect Raj Rewal – who had trained in Delhi and London and is one of the most distinguished of the second generation of Indian Modernists – completed a vast complex of exhibition pavilions in New Delhi for the international trade fair Asia 72. Making obvious references to the Crystal Palace of 1851, the complex was also intended to mark the 25th anniversary of Indian independence. Inaugurated by Nehru's daughter, prime minister Indira Gandhi, it was a final architectural symbol of the optimism of Nehru's post-independence India.

The largest of its four buildings, which resemble truncated Modernist pyramids, was the Hall of Nations. It was the world's first and largest-span space frame (78m/256ft) to be built in concrete, as steel was too expensive in India at the time. Around 300 families lived on site and built the complex in less than two years; 50 carpenters made the wooden boxes into which the concrete, carried up a bamboo scaffold in baskets, was hand-poured. The entire structure served as a 3D brise soleil to screen the sun and cool the building. 'It was designed as a sunbreaker,' Rewal explained. 'Le Corbusier put the sunbreaker on the outside, separate from the structure. Here it *is* the structure.'[5] This innovation was made possible by the Indian engineer Mahendra Raj, who had worked on Le Corbusier's Chandigarh's Capitol Complex as well as Charles Correa's Hindustan Lever Pavilion (1961), also in Pragati Maidan. Mahendra Raj's structural ingenuity enabled some of the striking forms of the modern architecture of post-independence India.

In the same complex was Rewal's Nehru Pavilion, an underground gallery that was the negative of these four larger structures, built to house an exhibition commemorating India's first prime minister. It had a raised mound inspired by Buddhist stupas, and a geometric plan reminiscent of mandalas, illustrative of the Indian Modernists' renewed interest in the country's architectural heritage. Rewal described it as 'Modern architecture

The Nehru Pavilion by Raj Rewal
featuring a memorial exhibition
by Charles and Ray Eames and the
National Institute of Design, 1972

with Indian roots. We appreciated traditional places in a modern way.'[6] The biographical exhibition inside the pavilion, *Jawaharlal Nehru: His Life and His India,* was designed by Charles and Ray Eames in collaboration with the National Institute of Design (NID), the institution that Nehru had helped found. It included portraits of Nehru as a Harrow schoolboy, a reconstruction of the prison cell in Ahmednagar Fort where he was incarcerated for his ninth spell from 1942 to 1945 (and where he wrote *The Discovery of India*) and large-scale photographs of the Bhakra Nangal Dam and other Modernist structures with which he was associated, including Chandigarh.

However, Nehru's vision of a secular, modern and progressive India is at odds with the trend of much contemporary Indian politics and the more assertive ethos of Hindu nationalism. In 2017 Raj Rewal's complex, including the memorial pavilion celebrating Nehru, was demolished overnight despite a vigorous campaign to save it. From the roof of Achyut Kanvinde's Nehru Science Centre, with its abstracted concrete *chhatris* that echo those of a nearby Mughal fort, one looks out over a redeveloped Pragati Maidan in which Rewal's iconic structure has been replaced by a bland campus designed for the 2023 G20 summit: a cluster of corporate buildings around a circular conference centre that is cruelly referred to as 'The Hamburger'. Other buildings, still standing, have been subject to thoughtless renovations, such as the lift shaft installed in Habib Rahman's Rabindra Bhavan, an arts centre that was almost co-designed with Nehru. As workmen disrespectfully smashed through one of its *jaali*-like screens to make way for the new lift, two cardboard cut-out figures of Narendra Modi stood nearby, as if silently approving of the destruction.

Much of Nehru's other Modernist architectural legacy is currently under threat, fragile monuments to independence and decolonization. At the chief architect's office in Chandigarh, a debate raged over whether Maxwell Fry's Kiran Cinema in Sector 22 should be saved or torn down to make way for a new multiplex. The overarching question is this: should the city be an open-air museum or able to change with the times? While Doshi's CEPT campus has recently been sensitively restored (using the opportunity presented by the closure of the university during COVID),

Looking from the
Hall of Nations
to the Halls of
Industry, Raj Rewal,
1970–4

students and faculty at the Indian Institute of Management have vacated Louis Kahn's badly maintained building, which rusty rebars and crumbling concrete have rendered unsafe. As a last-ditch campaign to save it is led by the alumni body and international architects and conservationists, the structure stands as eerily empty as a de Chirico painting. Le Corbusier's museum in Ahmedabad is also closed, supposedly to undergo restoration but with little evidence of any work having been done over the last few years.

Like Nehru, Prime Minister Modi styles himself 'the Architect of a New India', but his Bharatiya Janata Party (BJP) uses architecture to promote a Hindu nationalist rather than secular agenda. In 1951 Nehru insisted that the restoration of the Somnath temple in Gujarat be privately funded and that India's then president should attend its inauguration in a personal rather than official capacity; he chose to invest in his non-sectarian, industrial 'temples of Modern India' instead. Modi's government, by contrast, has financed expensive refurbishments of temples in Varanasi, Ayodhya and Ujjain as part of Modi's vision for a 'New India', a modern country (of Hindus) united by and able to build on its spiritual past. In January 2024 Modi controversially inaugurated a new £170m Hindu temple to the god Ram on the site of a sixteenth-century mosque in Ayodhya that was razed by nationalists in 1992.

Nehru once explored, with Gordon Cullen, the addition of Modernist buildings to Lutyens's ceremonial centre of New Delhi, with its colonial monuments and government buildings. He hoped to signal a new democratic direction, but apart from replacing colonial iconography with the Ashoka emblem, mostly the imperial aesthetics remained. Now Modi is redeveloping Lutyens's Central Vista, once known as 'Kingsway' or the Raj Path, which he describes as 'a symbol of slavery of the British Raj'.[7] In 2022 a massive statue of Subhas Chandra Bose, who collaborated with the Nazi government to fight for independence, was unveiled at India Gate, where a statue of George V once stood. New buildings designed by Modi's favoured architect Bimal Patel (his Albert Speer, but without the talent, according to artist Anish Kapoor) are intended to obliterate the colonial axis and mindset. Twelve

Model of the Nehru Pavilion
by Raj Rewal, 1972

landmark buildings are to be destroyed so that Modi can articulate his vision of a new, modern Indian cultural identity that many fear promotes a revisionist history and Hindu nationalist agenda. As part of the £1.4 billion scheme, which requires the demolition of India's National Museum, a new Parliament has been constructed next to the one designed by Herbert Baker, with interiors based on important Hindu symbols. It includes a mural of 'Akhand Bharat' (or 'undivided India'), a mythical Hindu civilization that unifies the Indian subcontinent.

While Nehru's legacy in India is being deliberately eroded – with the Nehru Museum and Library in his former residence at Teen Murti Bhavan transformed into a museum devoted to all former prime ministers, for example – the reputation of Nkrumah, long dismissed as a dictator and despot, is being restored. In 1977, as part of his rehabilitation, the statue of him outside Parliament House by Italian sculptor Nicola Cautaudella – which had been bombed before Queen Elizabeth II's visit in 1961 and then toppled in 1966 – was mounted on a new plinth in front of the National Museum Nkrumah commissioned for Accra. The statue lost both arms in the coup, but Nkrumah points to the future with phantom limbs, watched from behind by a statue of General Joseph Arthur Ankrah, the chair of the National Liberation Council who stabbed him in the back and replaced him as leader. A marble mausoleum by architect Don Arthur, who had studied architecture in Moscow, was completed in 1992; outside stands a golden statue of Nkrumah in the same pose but wearing kente, and heralded by crouching figures blowing elephant tusks, as they do in Ashanti royal processions. Another version of Cautadella's statue, also pulled down in 1966, stands behind the monument; beside it, Nkrumah's decapitated head is mounted on a separate plinth, almost as a cautionary tale about authoritarianism.

As in India, Tropical Modernist buildings are being lost in Ghana, with Fry and Drew's Community Centre at risk in the plans to redevelop Accra's foreshore and the derelict International Trade Fair site awaiting a new China-sponsored redevelopment. C.L.R. James, reflecting on Ghana's early years after independence, wrote that what he called the 'African degeneration' should not undermine the optimism of that early moment nor invalidate the promise that, as Nkrumah proclaimed, Africa was 'ready to fight its own battles and show that after all the black man is capable of managing his own affairs'.[8] Nkrumah, who perhaps betrayed that dream, is now recognized not only as a national hero, the founding father of Ghana, but as one of the most important Black leaders of the modern era. In our age of globalization and its consequences, many look back on the utopian possibilities of that immediate post-colonial moment and its architecture with nostalgia – and for inspiration.

Can Tropical Modernism, the architecture Nehru and Nkrumah appropriated and endorsed, and which embodied the ambitions they had for their new nations, be similarly rehabilitated? With many of its important buildings currently at risk from development and decay, can significant examples of Tropical Modernism be revalued and saved? How might new technologies provide enhanced data sets to help, and how can we make better use of local and sustainable materials and building construction techniques? How can a new generation of contemporary architects learn to design with climate in ways that lead on from where Tropical Modernism ended?

As we face an era of climate change, it is important that Tropical Modernism's scientifically informed principles of passive cooling are re-examined and reinvented for our age. Architects such as Anupama Kundoo, Bijoy Jain and Rahul Mehrotra in India and David Adjaye, Lesley Lokko, Francis Kéré and Kunlé Adeyemi in West Africa have been inspired by Tropical Modernism and its post-colonial adaptations. Following in the footsteps of trailblazing post-colonial architects, practitioners today look for sustainable solutions to increasingly extreme climates and continue to reflect on regional identities. Fusing scientific approaches with local knowledge, culture and materials, they seek to create a hopeful architectural future in South Asia and West Africa.

The Scott House by
Kenneth Scott, Accra, 1961

A dismembered statue of Nkrumah, behind which stands
another of General Joseph Arthur Ankrah, the Chair of
the National Liberation Council that deposed him

Notes

Introduction

1 'India: The New Mahatma', *Time*, 5 January 1959, citing Bombay's *Free Press Journal*.
2 Khilnani 2012, p.61.
3 Maxwell Fry, unpublished Autobiography, 'India', 1983, Fry and Drew Collection (14/6).
4 Maxwell Fry, 'Learning from the Tropics', recording at the Architecture Association, December 1979.
5 Mark Crinson in Bremner 2016, p.203. See also Jayewardene 2017, pp.126–7.
6 Gopal 2019, p.4.
7 Chen 2010, pp.3–4.

Chapter I

1 *The Gold Coast Handbook*, 1937, p.180. The book advises newcomers to West Africa on how to avoid disease and survive the hot conditions advising that, 'A good helmet, one containing an air space between two linings of aluminium foil, is essential and should be worn between 8a.m. and 4p.m. Crookes's tinted glasses are helpful in eliminating glare.'
2 Jane Drew, notes for unpublished Autobiography, Fry and Drew Collection (29/10).
3 Jane Drew, unpublished Autobiography, 'West Africa', Fry and Drew Collection (30/1), pp.69–70.
4 Jane Drew, Oral History, British Library, 1995.
5 *Architectural Association Journal*, January 1932, p.31.
6 *Architectural Association Journal*, January 1932, p.31.
7 Fry 1975, p.165.
8 Maxwell Fry, unpublished Autobiography, Fry and Drew Collection (14/2).
9 MacCarthy 2019, p.319.
10 MacCarthy 2019, p.291.
11 Mark Crinson in Bremner 2016, p.204.
12 Fry to Drew, 4 April 1943, Fry and Drew Collection (18/3).
13 Letter to Drew, 30 October 1944, Fry and Drew Collection (18/4).
14 Fry, unpublished Memoirs, Fry and Drew Collection (14/3; 14/2).
15 The idea of a *cordon sanitaire* was proposed by Frederic John Luggard. See Luggard 1926.
16 Fry, 'West Africa, the army', unpublished Memoir, Fry and Drew Collection (14/2), p.53.
17 Drew, Handwritten notes for an unpublished Autobiography, Fry and Drew Collection.
18 Fry, 'West Africa, the army', unpublished Autobiography, Fry and Drew Collection (14/2), p.6.
19 Fry, unpublished Autobiography, Fry and Drew Collection (14/3).
20 Fry, 'West Africa, the army', unpublished Memoir, Fry and Drew Collection (14/3), pp.57–8.
21 Fry citing Gropius, unpublished Autobiography, Fry and Drew Collection (14/2; 14/3). Jackson and Holland 2016, p.36.
22 Fry, 'West Africa, the army', unpublished Memoir, Fry and Drew Collection (14/3), p.62.
23 Maxwell Fry, 'Learning from the Tropics', recording at the Architecture Association, December 1979.
24 Jackson 2014.
25 Drew, 'West African Architecture', Fry and Drew Collection (29/1), p.78a.
26 Jackson and Holland 2016, p.156.
27 Fry, 'Learning from the Tropics', recording at the Architecture Association, December 1979. See also Patrick Zamarian, 'Global Perspectives and Private Concerns: The AA's Department of Tropical Architecture' (conference paper, 2 March 2021).
28 Uduku 2006, p.398.
29 Maxwell Fry, 'Learning from the Tropics', recording at the Architecture Association, December 1979.
30 *Maxwell Fry*, exhibition catalogue with a foreword by Nikolaus Pevsner, Monks Hall Museum, Eccles, June 1964, Fry and Drew Collection (12/13). See also Pevsner in Richards 1961.
31 Ogura 1986, pp.186–7.
32 'Koenigsberger: Early Years Abroad', interview with David Toppin, *Architect's Journal*, 7 July 1982, p.56.
33 Jane Drew, Oral History, British Library, 1995. See also von Osten 2014, p.18.
34 Gopal 2019, p.319.
35 Gopal 2019, p.7.
36 Hilde Marchant and John Deakin, 'Africa Speaks in Manchester', *Picture Post*, 10 November 1945.
37 Adi and Sherwood 1995, p.165.
38 Padmore 1963, p.v.
39 Davidson 2019, p.47.
40 Davidson 2019, p.86.
41 Kwami 2013, p.50. See also Antubam 1963.
42 Jackson and Holland 2016, p.194.
43 Bradley 1955, p.9.
44 Harold Macmillan's speech in Accra, 9 January 1960, in Butler and Stockwell 2013, p.2.

Chapter II

1 McArthur 1992, pp. 234–7.
2 Brass 2003, 2006.
3 Ahluwalia 2019, p.158.
4 Prakash 2023, p.10.
5 Gopal 2019, p.239.
6 Khilnani 2012, p.123.
7 Lutyens quoted in Burroughs and Stockwell 2013, p.79.
8 Nehru, 1950, quoted in Kalia 2006, pp.133–56.
9 Flint 2014, p.148.
10 Fry, 'India', unpublished Autobiography, Fry and Drew Collection (14/6).
11 Drew, 'India', unpublished Autobiography, Fry and Drew Collection (30/1), p.114.
12 Fry, 'India', unpublished Autobiography, Fry and Drew Collection (14/6).
13 Flint 2014, p.149.
14 Khilnani 2012, p.131.
15 Casciato, Nievergelt, Scheidegger, von Moos 2010, p.27.
16 Drew, 'People', Fry and Drew Collection (29/3) p.166. See also Drew, 'Le Corbusier', Fry and Drew Collection (29/2).
17 Casciato, Nievergelt, Scheidegger, von Moos 2010, p.29.
18 Fry, 'Le Corbusier at Chandigarh' quoted in Khilnani 2012, p.132.
19 Correa in Correa 1996, p.59.
20 Drew, 'Chandigarh', Fry and Drew Collection (29/6), p.3.
21 Drew, Fry and Drew Collection (29/3).
22 Le Corbusier 1995, *Oeuvre complète*. Vol. VI, p.51.
23 Le Corbusier 1995, *Oeuvre complète*. *Les dernières œuvre*, p.76. See also Siret 2006.
24 Jackson and Holland 2016, p.230.
25 Prakash, 2002, p.19.
26 Nehru 1994, p.50.
27 Le Corbusier to Nehru, quoted in Stanislaus von Moos, 'The Politics of the Open Hand: Notes on Le Corbusier and Nehru at Chandigarh', in Walden 2021, p.46.
28 Ackley 2006.
29 Flint 2014, p.153.
30 Walden 2021, p.398.
31 Drew, 'Chandigarh', Fry and Drew Collection (29/6), p.3.
32 *Marg* magazine, vol. 15, Issue 1, 1961.
33 Bremner 2016, p.206.
34 Khan, 1987, p.15.
35 Author interview with Shivdatt Sharma, October 2023.
36 Drew, 'India', Fry and Drew Collection (30/1), p.116.
37 Casciato, Nievergelt, Scheidegger, von Moos 2010, p.31.
38 Khilnani 2012, p.132.
39 Bhaga 2000, p.117.
40 Tim McQuirk, 'Le Corbusier's Punjabi Dream', *The Independent*, 3 March 1996.
41 Prakash 2019, p.63.
42 Prakash 2002, p.151.
43 Prakash 2002, pp.151–2.
44 Drew 1963, p.57–8.
45 Author interview with Jeet Malhotra, January 2020.
46 Jane Drew, Oral History, British Library, 1995.

47 Prakash and Sharma 2012, p.8.
48 Doshi foreword to Prakash and Sharma 2012, p.8.
49 Author interview with Shivdatt Sharma, October 2023.
50 Drew, 'India', Fry and Drew Collection (30/1), p.113.
51 Casciato, Nievergelt, Scheidegger, von Moos 2010, p.35.
52 Author interview with Jaswinder Singh, October 2023.
53 M.N. Sharma in Wattas and Gandhi 2018, p.207.
54 M.N. Sharma in Wattas and Gandhi 2018, p.207.
55 Author interview with Jaswinder Singh, October 2023.
56 M.N. Sharma in Wattas and Gandhi 2018, p.208.

Chapter III

1 Nkrumah, Independence Speech, 6 March 1957, Accra, *Ghana*. BBC World Service | Focus On Africa | "Ghana is free forever".
2 Stanek 2020, p.46.
3 Nkrumah, speech at the founding of the Organization of African Unity (OAU), Addis Ababa, 24 May 1963. It became the title of his book *Africa Must Unite* (1964).
4 Harold Macmillan's speech in Accra, 9 January 1960, in Butler and Stockwell 2013, p.2.
5 Nkrumah 1961, pp. xi–xiv.
6 'Champ's African "Love Affair"', *Ebony* magazine, September 1964.
7 Nkrumah, All-African People's Conference, Government Printer, 1959, p.6.
8 Lentz 2017, pp.551–82.
9 Nkrumah: I Am No Dictator, *Daily Graphic*, Issue 2098, 21 June 1957, p.1.
10 This is the New Ghana Kwame Nkrumah is Building, *Evening News*, Tuesday 21 May 1963, p.6.
11 Powell 1984, p.145.
12 Powell 1984, p.145.
13 Miescher 2022, Part 2, p.120.

14 'India: The New Mahatma', *Time*, 5 January 1959.
15 Latham 2011, p.84.
16 Obeng 1961, p.189.
17 Latham 2011, p.68.
18 Jackson 2022, p.302.
19 Jackson 2022, p.309.
20 Michael Hirst, unpublished memoir, 2009.
21 Michael Hirst, unpublished memoir, 2009.
22 'The Role of Constantinos Doxiadis in the Development of the Master Plan 2 for Tema, Ghana', *Athens Journal* (2022), p.5.
23 Koenigsberger, 'Proposal to the Ford Foundation for the establishment of a Department of Development Studies at the Architecture Association, London', 1965–6, AA Archives.
24 Author interview with Ola Uduku, March 2023.
25 Stanek 2020, p.59. See also Stanek 2022.
26 Chitty 1958, p.400.
27 'Fry and Drew Papers, 'People' (29/3), pp.175–6. See also Buckminster Fuller at KNUST '64, Faculty of Architecture, Occasional Report, No.3, 1965.
28 Lloyd 1966, p.4.
29 Addo and Bond 1966, p.26.
30 Voice of America interview with E.T. Mensah, December 1981. See also Plageman 2013.
31 Author interview with John Owusu Addo, January 2023.
32 Author interview with Henry Wellington, February 2023.
33 Author interview with Patrick Wakely, March 2023. See also Wakely 1983.
34 Lloyd, 'Challenge', University Press, KNUST, Kumasi, May 1965 (pamphlet for the International Union of Architects Conference on Architectural Education, Paris 1965).

Chapter IV

1 Khilnani 2012, p.134.
2 Sherman 2022, p.192.

3 Nehru, 'Opening Remarks at the International Exhibition on Low-Cost Housing by the Prime Minister: 25 October 1953', Exhibition Souvenir, New Delhi, India, 1954.
4 Prakash 2002, p.11.
5 Chakrabarti 2013, p.170.
6 Batley in lecture delivered at the Indian Institute of Architects on 4 October 1934. Cited by Mustansir Dalvi, 'Contemporary Voices on Bombay's Architecture before the Nation State' (Art Deco Mumbai, 2020).
7 Manifesto of the Ceylon Reform Society founded by Coomaraswamy, quoted in Jayewardene 2017, p.24.
8 Nehru 1994, p.59.
9 Kabir, Humayun, in Kanvinde 1959, pp.1–4.
10 Nehru, in Kanvinde 1959, pp.5–9.
11 Nehru, in Kanvinde 1959, pp.5–9.
12 Nehru, in Kanvinde 1959, pp.5–9.
13 Author interview with Ram Rahman, January 2024.
14 Khilnani 2012, p.171.
15 Prakash 2002, p.25.
16 Curtis 1986, p.202.
17 Doshi in Emanuel 2016, p.211.
18 Prakash quoted in Barbara Corssette, 'Le Corbusier's Chandigarh', *New York Times*, 25 April 1982, Section 10, p.21.
19 Prakash 2019, p.5.
20 Sharma in Wattas and Gandhi 2018, p.206.
21 Sharma in Wattas and Gandhi 2018, p.206.
22 Takhar 2002, pp.79–80.
23 Bhatti 2018.
24 'Nek Chand: An Early Encounter', *Raw Vision* 35 (summer 2001), p.28.
25 Fry, Le Corbusier at Chandigarh, in Walden 1977, p.12.
26 Jackson 2002, p.54.

Epilogue

1 Stanek 2020, p.36.
2 Hess 2006, p.182. See also, Walter 1965, p.115.
3 Apter 1968, p. 30.

4 Fry and Drew Papers, 'West African Architecture' (29/3), p.78c.
5 Author interview with Raj Rewal, September 2023.
6 Author interview with Raj Rewal, September 2023.
7 'Rajpath, symbol of slavery, is now history: Modi at Central Vista avenue inauguration', *Indian Express*, 9 September 2022.
8 Getachew 2019, p.1.

Archives

In researching and writing this book, I have consulted archives in the UK at the Royal Institute of British Architects (RIBA) where the Fry and Drew Collection is held (some files of which only opened in 2020), the Architectural Association (AA), National Archives, the Working Class Movement Library, Churchill Archives Centre / Cambridge, University of Westminster, and the British Library; in Ghana, at the Ghana Institute of Architects (GIA), George Padmore Research Library, Kwame Nkrumah University of Science and Technology (KNUST), Bailey's African History Archive, and Deo Gratias; in India at Chandigarh College of Architecture (CCA), Chief-Architect's Office / Chandigarh, Centre for Environmental Planning and Technology (CEPT), National Institute of Design (NID); and in North America at the Avery Library, Columbia University and the Canadian Centre for Architecture (CCA).

Bibliography

Ackley 2006
Brian Ackley, 'Le Corbusier's Algerian Fantasy', *Bidoun*, Winter 2006

Addo and Bond 1966
John Owusu Addo and J. Max Bond, 'Aspirations', *Arena: The Architectural Association Journal*, Kumasi special issue, Journal 82, 1966

Adjaye and Allison 2016
David Adjaye and Peter Allison, *Adjaye, Africa, Architecture: A Photographic Survey of Metropolitan Architecture* (London 2016)

Ahluwalia 2019
Mallika Ahluwalia, *Divided by Partition, United by Resilience: 21 Inspirational Stories from 1947* (New Delhi 2019)

Alagiah 2008
George Alagiah, *A Passage to Africa* (London 2008)

Anderson 2021
Warwick Anderson, 'Decolonizing the Foundation of Tropical Architecture', *ABE Journal*, no. 18

Antubam 1963
Kofi Antubam, *Ghana's Heritage of Culture* (Leipzig 1963)

Apter 1968
David E. Apter, 'Nkrumah, Charisma, and the Coup', *Daedalus* 97 (3): 757–92.

Avermaete, Karakayali and Von Osten 2010
Tom Avermaete, Serhat Karakayali and Marion Von Osten. *Colonial Modern: Aesthetics of the Past, Rebellions for the Future* (London 2010)

Bader 2019
Vera Simone Bader, *Balkrishna Doshi, Writings on Architecture & Identity* (Berlin 2019)

Bagha and Bagha 2000
Sarbjit Bagha and Surinder Bagha, *Le Corbusier and Pierre Jeanneret: Footprints on the Sands of Indian Architecture* (Delhi 2000)

Balaara, Haarhoff and Melis 2018
Allan Stephen Balaara, Errol Haarhoff and Alessandro Melis, 'J. Max Bond Jr. and the Appropriation of Modernism in a Library Design in Ghana', *Fabrications* 28 (3): 355–74

Baweja, Bing and Veikos 2007
Vandana Baweja, Judith Bing and Cathrine Veikos. 'The Beginning of a Green Architecture: Otto Koenigsberger at the Department of Tropical Architecture at the Architectural Association (AA) School of Architecture, London, UK', *Association of Collegiate Schools of Architecture* 8 (Jan)

Berre, Geissler and Lagae 2022
Nina Berre, Paul Wenzel Geissler and Johan Lagae, *African Modernism and Its Afterlives* (Bristol 2022)

Bhatt and Scriver 1990
Vikram Bhatt and Peter Scriver, *After the Masters* (Washington 1990)

Bhatti 2018
S.S. Bhatti, *Rock Garden in Chandigarh: A Critical Evaluation of the Work of Nek Chand* (London 2018)

Bhatti 2019
S.S. Bhatti, *Shiv Datt Sharma: Life and Work* (London 2019)

Blazwick 2001
Iwona Blazwick (ed.), *Century City: Art and Culture in the Modern Metropolis* (London 2001)

Bourret 1961
F.M. Bourret, *Ghana, the Road to Independence, 1919–1957* (Lagos 1961)

Bradley 1955
Kenneth Bradley, *Britain's Purpose in Africa* (London 1955)

Brass 2003
Paul R. Brass, 'The Partition of India and Retributive Genocide in the Punjab, 1946–47: Means, Methods, and Purposes', *Journal of Genocide Research* 5 (1): 71–101

Brass 2006
Paul R. Brass, *Forms of Collective Violence: Riots, Pogroms and Genocide in Modern India* (Gurgaon 2006)

Bremmer 2016
G.A. Bremner (ed.), *Architecture and Urbanism in the British Empire* (Oxford 2016)

Burroughs and Stockwell 2013
Peter Burroughs and A.J. Stockwell, *Managing the Business of Empire* (London 2013)

Butler and Stockwell 2013
L.J. Butler and Sarah Stockwell, *The Wind of Change: Harold Macmillan and British Decolonization* (Basingstoke 2013)

Casciato, Nievergelt, Scheidegger, von Moos 2010
Maristella Casciato, Verena Nievergelt, Ernst Scheidegger and Stanislaus von Moos, *Chandigarh 1956: Le Corbusier, Pierre Jeanneret, Jane B. Drew, E. Maxwell Fry* (Zurich 2010)

Chakrabarti 2013
Vibhuti Chakrabarti, *Indian Architectural Theory and Practice* (London 2013)

Chen 2010
Kuan-Hsing Chen, *Asia as Method: Towards Deimperialization* (Durham, North Carolina 2010)

Chitty 1958
Anthony M. Chitty, 'The Need for Regionalism in Architecture: A Ghana Aesthetic?', *The Builder* CXCV (1958): 400

Correa 1996
Charles Correa and Kenneth Frampton, *Charles Correa* (London 1996)

Crowder, Fage and Oliver 1995
Michael Crowder, John Donnelly Fage and Roland Anthony Oliver, *The Cambridge History of Africa: vol. 8, from c.1940 to c.1975* (Cambridge 1995)

Curtis 1986
William J R. Curtis, *Raj Rewal* (Milan and Paris 1986)

Das 2013
Shilpa Das (ed.), *50 Years of the National Institute of Design, 1961–2011* (Ahmedabad 2013)

Davidson 2019
Basil Davidson, *Black Star* (London 2019)

Drew 1963
Jane Drew, 'Indigenous Architecture: Architecture in the Tropics', *Perspecta*, 8

Drew, Fry and Ford 2013
Jane Drew, Maxwell Fry and Harry L. Ford, *Village Housing in the Tropics* (London 2013)

Emanuel 2016
Muriel Emanuel, *Contemporary Architects* (Berlin 2016)

Evenson 1966
Norma Evenson, *Chandigarh* (Berkley & Los Angeles 1966)

Feiersinger and Vass 2015
Werner Feiersinger and Andreas Vass, *Chandigarh Redu: Le Corbusier, Pierre Jeanneret, Jane B. Drew, E. Maxwell Fry* (Zurich 2015)

Flint 2014
Anthony Flint, *Modern Man: The Life of Le Corbusier, Architect of Tomorrow* (Boston 2014)

Foyle 1954
Arthur M. Foyle and University College, *Conference on Tropical Architecture ... A Report of the Proceedings of the Conference Held at University College* (London 1953)

Fry 1969
Maxwell Fry, *Art in a Machine Age: A Critique of Contemporary Life Through the Medium of Architecture* (London 1969)

Fry 1975
Maxwell Fry, *Autobiographical Sketches* (London 1975)

Fry and Drew 1964
Maxwell Fry and Jane Drew, *Tropical Architecture in the Humid Zone* (London 1964)

Getachew 2019
Adom Getachew, *Worldmaking After Empire: The Rise and Fall of Self-Determination* (Princeton 2019)

Gopal 2019
Priyamvada Gopal, *Insurgent Empire: Anticolonial Resistance and British Dissent* (London and New York 2019)

Hakim, Sherwood and Padmore 1995
Adi Hakim, Marika Sherwood and George Padmore, *The 1945 Manchester Pan-African Congress Revisited* (London 1995)

Havinden and Meredith 1993
Michael Ashley Havinden and David Meredith (eds), *Colonialism and Development: Britain and Its Tropical Colonies, 1850-1960* (London and New York 1993)

Herz, Schröder, Focketyn and Jamrozik 2015
Manuel Herz, Ingrid Schröder, Hans Focketyn and Julia Jamrozik, *African Modernism* (Zurich 2015)

Hess 2006
Janet Hess, *Art and Architecture in Postcolonial Africa* (Jefferson 2006)

Hitchins 1978
Stephen Hitchins, *Fry, Drew, Knight, Creamer* (London 1978)

Ince and Johnson 2018
Catherine Ince, Lotte Johnson and Barbican Art Gallery, *The World of Charles and Ray Eames* (London 2018)

Jackson 2002
Iain Jackson, 'Politicised Territories: Nek Chand's Rock Garden', *GBER* 2.2

Jackson 2013
Iain Jackson, 'Tropical Architecture and the West Indies: From Military Advances and Tropical Medicine, to Robert Gardner-Medwin and the Networks of Tropical Modernism', *The Journal of Architecture* 18 (2): 167–95

Jackson 2014
Iain Jackson, 'Tropical Modernism: Fry and Drew's African Experiment', *Architectural Review*, 4 July 2014

Jackson 2022
Iain Jackson, 'Development Visions in Ghana: From Design Schools and Building Research to Tema New Town', *Architectural History* 65 (2022)

Jackson and Holland 2016
Iain Jackson and Jessica Holland, *The Architecture of Edwin Maxwell Fry and Jane Drew* (London 2016)

Jackson and Oppong 2014
Iain Jackson and Rexford Assasie Oppong, 'The Planning of Late Colonial Village Housing in the Tropics: Tema Manhean, Ghana', *Planning Perspectives* 29 (4): 475–99

Jayewardene 2017
Shanti Jayewardene, *Geoffrey Manning Bawa: Decolonising Architecture* (Colombo 2017)

Joshi 1999
Kiran Joshi, *Documenting Chandigarh: The Indian Architecture of Pierre Jeanneret, Edwin Maxwell Fry, Jane Beverly Drew* (Ahmedabad 1999)

Kalia 2006
Ravi Kalia, 'Modernism, Modernization and Post-Colonial India: A Reflective Essay', *Planning Perspectives* 21 (2): 133–56

Kanvinde 1959
Achyut Kanvinde, Achyut (ed.), *Seminar on Architecture* (New Delhi 1959)

Khan 1987
Hasan-Uddin Khan, *Charles Correa* (Architects in the Third World) (New York 1987)

Khan 2007
Yasmin Khan, *The Great Partition: The Making of India and Pakistan* (New Haven 2007)

Khan, Beinart and Correa 2009
Hasan-Uddin Khan, Julian Beinart and Charles Correa, *Le Corbusier: Chandigarh and the Modern City: Insights into the Iconic City Sixty Years Later* (Ahmedabad 2009)

Khilnani 2012
Sunil Khilnani, *The Idea of India* (London 2012)

Kwami 2013
Atta Kwami, *Kumasi Realism, 1951–2007: An African Modernism* (London 2013)

Lang, Desai and Desai 2000
Jon Lang, Madhavi Desai and Miki Desai, *Architecture and Independence: The Search for Identity – India 1880 to 1980* (Delhi and Oxford 2000)

Latham 2011
Michael E. Latham, *The Right Kind of Revolution: Modernization, Development, and U.S. Foreign Policy from the Cold War to the Present* (Ithaca, NY 2011)

Le Corbusier 1995
Le Corbusier, *Oeuvre complète en 8 volumes* ed. Willy Boesiger (Berlin and Boston 1995)

Lentz 2017
Carola Lentz, 'Ghanaian "Monument Wars": The Contested History of the Nkrumah Statues', September 2017, *Cahiers d études africaines* 52(3): 551–82

Liscombe 2006
Rhodri Windsor Liscombe, 'Modernism in Late Imperial British West Africa: The Work of Maxwell Fry and Jane Drew, 1946-56', *Journal of the Society of Architectural Historians* 65 (2): 188–215

Lloyd 1966
John (Michael) Lloyd, 'Intentions', *Arena: The Architecture Association Journal*, Kumasi special issue, 32 (July/August): 4

Lokko 2023
Lesley Lokko (ed.), *Biennale Architettura 2023. The Laboratory of the Future*, Catalogue, La Biennale di Venezia (Milan 2023)

Lu 2011
Duanfang Lu, *Third World*

Modernism: Architecture, Development and Identity (London 2011)

Luggard 1926
Frederic John Luggard, *The Dual Mandate in British Tropical Africa* (Edinburgh and London 1926)

Lutyens 1981
Lutyens, the Work of the English Architect Sir Edwin Lutyens (1869–1944), exh. cat., Hayward Gallery (London 1981)

MacCarthy 2019
Fiona MacCarthy, *Walter Gropius: Visionary Founder of the Bauhaus* (London 2019)

McArthur 1992
Brian McArthur, *Penguin Book of Twentieth Century Speeches* (London 1992)

Maxwell 1975
Edwin Maxwell, *Autobiographical Sketches* (London 1975)

Maxwell 1937
Sir John Maxwell, *The Gold Coast Handbook, 1937* (London and Worcester 1937)

Mehta, Mehndiratta and Huber 2016
Vandini Mehta, Rohit Raj Mehndiratta and Ariel Huber, *The Structure: Works of Mahendra Raj* (Zurich 2016)

Meuser and Dalbai 2021
Philipp Meuser and Adil Dalbai, *Architectural Guide. Sub-Saharan Africa. Volume 3 Western Africa: Along the Atlantic Ocean Coast* (Berlin 2021)

Miescher 2022
Stephan F. Miescher, *A Dam for Africa* (Bloomington 2022)

Mitter 2007
Partha Mitter, *The Triumph of Modernism: Indian Artists and the Avante-Garde, 1922–1947* (London 2007)

Nehru 1994
Jawaharlal Nehru, *The Discovery of India* (New Delhi 1994)

Nehru 2004
Jawaharlal Nehru, *Jawaharlal Nehru: An Autobiography* (New Delhi 2004)

Nkrumah 1961
Kwame Nkrumah, *I Speak of Freedom* (New York 1961)

Nkrumah 1962
Kwame Nkrumah, *Towards Colonial Freedom* (London 1962)

Nkrumah 1964
Kwame Nkrumah, *Africa Must Unite* (London 1964)

Nkrumah 1965
Kwame Nkrumah, *Neo-Colonialism: The Last Stage of Imperialism* (London 1965)

Nkrumah 1969
Kwame Nkrumah, *Handbook of Revolutionary Warfare* (New York 1969)

Obeng 1961
Samuel Obeng (ed.), *Selected Speeches of Dr. Kwame Nkrumah, First President of the Republic of Ghana*, vol. 2 (Accra 1961)

Oforiatta-Ayim 2019
Nana Oforiatta-Ayim and Biennale De Venise, *Ghana Freedom: Ghana Pavilion at the 58th International Art Exhibition-La Biennale Di Venezia* (London 2019)

Ogura 1986
Nobuyuki Ogura, 'Postwar Modern Movement in West Africa and British Architects', *Journal of Architecture, Planning and Environmental Engineering* 368 (October 1986): 185–93

Padmore 1963
George Padmore, *History of the Pan-African Congress* (London 1963)

Peiry, Maizels and Lespinasse 2006
Lucienne Peiry, John Maizels and Philippe Lespinasse, *Nek Chand's Outsider Art* (Paris 2006)

Pevsner 1964
Nikolaus Pevsner, *Maxwell Fry*, exh. cat., Monks Hall Museum, Eccles, June 1964

Plageman 2013
Nate Plageman, *Highlife Saturday Night* (Bloomington 2013)

Platts 1966
Beryl Platts, 'The Architect as Collector: The Modern Collection of Maxwell Fry and Jane Drew', *Country Life*, vol. 140 (26 September 1966)

Powell 1984
Erica Powell, *Private Secretary (Female)/Gold Coast* (London 1984)

Prakash 1978
Aditya Prakash, *Chandigarh: a presentation in free verse* (Chandigarh 1978)

Prakash 2002
Vikramaditya Prakash, *Chandigarh's Le Corbusier: The Struggle for Modernity in Postcolonial India* (Studies in Modernity and National Identity) (Washington 2002)

Prakash 2019
Vikramaditya Prakash, *One Continuous Line: Art, Architecture and Urbanism of Aditya Prakash* (Ahmedabad 2019)

Prakash 2023
Vikramaditya Prakash, *Le Corbusier's Chandigarh Revisited* (London 2023)

Prakash and Sharma 2012
Vikramaditya Prakash and Shivdatt Sharma, *The Architecture of Shivdatt Sharma* (Ahmedabad 2012)

Prouvé and d'Ayot 2006
Jean Prouvé and Catherine Dumont d'Ayot, *Jean Prouvé: The Poetics of the Technical Object* (Weil am Rhein 2006)

Rewal and Jahanbegloo 2019
Raj Rewal and Ramin Jahanbegloo, *Talking Architecture* (New Delhi and Oxford 2019)

Rhomberg and Bittner et al. 2013
Kathrin Rhomberg and Regina Bittner et al., *The Bauhaus in Calcutta* (Ostfildern 2013)

Richards 1961
James Maude Richards (ed.),

New Buildings in the Commonwealth [Reprinted from Special Numbers of the Architectural Review, with Additional Material] (London 1961)

le Roux 2003
Hannah le Roux, 'The Networks of Tropical Architecture', *The Journal of Architecture* 8 (3): 337–54

le Roux 2004(a)
Hannah le Roux, 'Modern Architecture in Post-Colonial Ghana and Nigeria', *Architectural History* 47 (47): 361–92

le Roux 2004(b)
Hannah le Roux, 'Building on the Boundary – Modern Architecture in the Tropics', *Social Identities* 10 (4): 439–53

Scriver and Prakash 2007
Peter Scriver and Vikramaditya Prakash, *Colonial Modernities* (London 2007)

Sharma 2023
Shivdatt Sharma, *Pierre Jeanneret and Chandigarh* (New Delhi 2023)

Sherman 2022
Taylor C. Sherman, *Nehru's India: A History in Seven Myths* (Princeton and Oxford 2022)

Singh, Mukherjee and Kapoor 2009
Malvika Singh, Rudrangshu Mukherjee and Pramod Kapoor, *New Delhi, Making of a Capital* (New Delhi 2009)

Siret 2006
Daniel Siret, *Le Corbusier Plans. 1950 – Studies in Sunlight*

– *Tower of Shadows (Chandigarh)* (Fondation Le Corbusier 2006)

Spivak 2003
Gayatri Chakravorty Spivak, *A Critique of Postcolonial Reason: Toward a History of the Vanishing Present* (Cambridge, Mass. 2003)

Stanek 2020
Łukasz Stanek, *Architecture in Global Socialism: Eastern Europe, West Africa, and the Middle East in the Cold War* (Princeton 2020)

Stanek 2022
Łukasz Stanek, 'Post-Colonial Education in Kumasi', *Architectural Review*, 20 September 2022

Steele 1998
James Steele, *The Complete Architecture of Balkrishna Doshi* (London 1998)

Stierli et al. 2022
Martino Stierli, Anoma Pieris, Sean Anderson and Art New, *The Project of Independence: Architectures of Decolonization in South Asia, 1947–1985* (New York 2022)

Takhar 2002
Jaspreet Takhar, *Celebrating Chandigarh* (Ahmedabad 2002)

Uduku 2006
Ola Uduku, 'Modernist Architecture and "the Tropical" in West Africa: The Tropical Architecture Movement in West Africa, 1948–1970', *Habitat International* 30 (3): 396–411

Vale 2008
Lawrence Vale, *Architecture, Power, and National Identity* (London 2008)

von Osten 2014
Marion von Osten, *A Hot Topic: Tropical Architecture and its Aftermath* (New York 2014)

von Tunzelmann 2012
Alex von Tunzelmann, *Indian Summer* (London 2012)

Wakely 1983
Pat Wakely, 'The Development of a school: An account of the Department of development and tropical studies of the Architectural association 1953–1972', *Habitat International*, vol. 7, no. 5–6.

Walden 2021
Russell Walden, *The Open Hand: Essays on Le Corbusier* (Massachusetts 2021)

Walter 1965
Peter Walter, *Kwame Nkrumah and Africa* (London 1965)

Wattas and Gandhi 2018
Rajnish Wattas and Deepika Gandhi (eds), *Le Corbusier Rediscovered: Chandigarh and beyond* (New Delhi 2018)

Acknowledgements

Many thanks to my co-curator of the V&A's 2024 *Tropical Modernism: Architecture and Independence* exhibition, Justine Sambrook, and my co-curators of the *Tropical Modernism: Architecture and Power in West Africa* exhibition at the 2023 Venice Architecture Biennale, Nana Biamah-Ofosu and Bushra Mohamed. Their expertise has been invaluable and they have been fantastic colleagues.

The idea for this project had its origins in a 2018 trip to Sri Lanka, where I toured Geoffrey Bawa's and Minnette de Silva's buildings armed with Shanti Jayewardene's excellent book *Geoffrey Manning Bawa: Decolonizing Architecture* (2017) and learned about Maxwell Fry and Jane Drew and the Department of Tropical Architecture at the Architectural Association. Many thanks to my other guides there: Madhura Prematilleke, Veranjan Kurukulasuriya and Anoma Wijewardene.

In the UK, there is a good deal of scholarly expertise on Tropical Modernism and its period, and I have benefited from the help and advice of critical friends including Ola Uduku, Mark Crinson, Łukasz Stanek, Albert Brenchat Aguilar, Patrick Zamarian, Inigo Thomas, Michael Hirst, Patrick Wakely, Shahed Saleem, Lesley Lokko and especially Iain Jackson.

For help in India, my gratitude to Rajshree Pathy, a wonderful host, Feroze Gujral, Ram Rahman, Sunil Khilnani, Raj Rewal, Jeet Malhotra, Shivdatt Sharma, Madhu Sarin, Kiran Nadar, Roobina Karode, Depeeka Ghandi, Sangeeta Bagga, Jaswinder Singh, Kapil Setia, Sanjay Kanvinde, Naeem Mohaiemen, Asim Waqif, Diwan Manna, Rohit Raj, Abhay Mangaldas, Surit Sarabhai, Snehal Shah, Sunaina Shah, Tanishka Kachuru, Kishwar Desai, Kartikeya Shodhan and Vikramaditya Prakash.

For Ghana, I'm indebted to John Owusu Addo, Henry Wellington, Samia Nkrumah, David Adjaye, Kojo Derban, Patience Larbi, Korantemaa Larbi, Nana Oforiatta Ayim, George Insiful, Samuel Afram, Divine Owusu-Ansah, Victoria Cooke, Charlie Laing, Marwan Zakhem, Penelope Troy, Kuukuwa Manful, Geta Striggner-Scott, Joe Osae-Addo, Kingsley Ofosu-Ntiamoah, Nate Plageman, John Akomfrah and James Barnor.

Thanks to Daniel Duah, Alexander Marful, Rexford Assasie Oppong, Isaac Kwofie Egyir and Christian Koranteng at Kwame Nkrumah University of Science and Technology; to Ingrid Schroder, Ed Bottoms, Amy Finn and Golnar Tajdar at the Architectural Association; and to Charles Hind, Fiona Orsini and Oliver Urquhart-Irvine at RIBA, and to Shireen Mahdavi for access to the Fry and Drew Collection.

Also, to Tristram Hunt for his unwavering belief in this project, Coralie Hepburn at V&A Publishing for helping to shape this book, to the Graham Foundation for a generous grant, and to Claire Thomas for encourage-ment and support, covering for long periods of travel abroad and nursing me through bouts of malaria at home.

Index

Illustrations and captions are denoted by the use of italic page numbers.

Picture Credits

Achaempomg – Photo Base, Accra; unknown

134–6 Photo: Michael Hirst

137 (above) Photo: Victoria and Albert Museum, London; (below) Courtesy Manuela Nebuloni and Postbox Ghana / Photo: Film Base, Accra

138 Photo: Courtesy Michael and Catherine Lloyd / Source: Monica Pacheco – 'War Transnational Consultants in Housing and Planning Development Narratives: The Case of Otto Koenigsberger'

139 (above) Photo: Patrick Wakely (Professor Emeritus, University of London); (below) Photo: © Keith Critchlow Legacy CIC / Courtesy Architectural Association Archives, London

140 Courtesy Architectural Association Archives, London

141 Photo: Patrick Wakely (Professor Emeritus, University of London)

142–3 J. Max Bond Jr. papers, 1955–2009, Avery Architectural & Fine Arts Library, Columbia University

144 Photo: Patrick Wakely (Professor Emeritus, University of London)

146–7 Kwame Nkrumah University of Science and Technology, KNUST – Kamasi

148–55 Film stills from *Tropical Modernism: Architecture and Power in West Africa*, © Victoria and Albert Museum, London / Photo: Charlie Laing

156 Courtesy Sanjay Kanvide

158–9 © Edmund Sumner

160 Courtesy Ram Rahman

166–7 Photo: Iwan Baan

168 Photo: Victoria and Albert Museum, London

171 Photo: Habib Rahman, courtesy Ram Rahman

172–3 Photo: Courtesy Randhir Singh

175 © University of Westminster Archive / Gordon Cullen Estate

176 Photo: Republic News Pictures, New Delhi

177 Photo: Habib Rahman, courtesy Ram Rahman

178 © Manuel Bougot

180–3 Courtesy Vastushilpa Foundation

184–5 © Estate of Aditya Prakash / Photo: Canadian Centre for Architecture

186 Photo: Travel / Alamy Stock Photo

188 Photo: Victoria and Albert Museum, London

190–1 © Edmund Sumner

192 Courtesy Raj Rewal

198–9 © Edmund Sumner

200 Photo: Courtesy Madan Mahatta Archives & PHOTOINK

202–3 Film stills from *Tropical Modernism: Architecture and Power in West Africa*, © Victoria and Albert Museum, London / Photo: Charlie Laing

204 Photo: World History Archive / Alamy Stock Photo

207 National Institute of Design-Archive, Ahmedabad

208–9 © Raj Rewal. Photo: Georges Meguerditchian – Centre Pompidou, MNAM-CCI /Dist. RMN-GP

210 © Raj Rewal

212–13 Film stills from *Tropical Modernism: Architecture and Power in West Africa*,

© Victoria and Albert Museum, London / Photo: Charlie Laing